# CANAL DAYS IN SWINDON

## by Dr. Eric V. Tull

ISBN 0 9521156 0 3

Cover Layout and Design by Derek Winterbottom
Printed by Parkes and Mainwarings Limited
41 Gt. Lister St., Birmingham B7 4LP

# ACKNOWLEDGEMENTS

The author gratefully acknowledges the invaluable help given by the late Mr L J Dalby, Mr M J Stone, the late Mr C Tapscott-Mason, Mr J Harber and Mr F G Bellamy, together with various members of the Swindon Society and numerous private individuals and local companies who have contributed to the compilation of this record.

The cooperation and helpfulness of the staff of Swindon Reference Library, the Railway Museum, the Swindon Museum, the Wiltshire County Records Office, the Air Photographs Office of the Department of the Environment, and the Archaeology Division of the Ordnance Survey, Southampton has made the task of amassing the evidence much easier.

Fig. 1 is reproduced from the Victoria County History of Wiltshire Vol. IX by permission of the General Editor of the Victoria County History.

Figs. 2, 3, 6, 10, 25 and 32 are reproduced from the Swindon Museum Collection, with the permission of the Curator.

Figs. 11, 20, 21 and 30 are reproduced from originals held by Swindon Reference Library with the permission of the Wiltshire County Council Library and Museum Service.

Figs. 28 and 29 are reproduced from the 1886 Ordnance Survey Maps, 1/2500 Series, with the permission of the Ordnance Survey.

Fig. 27 is reproduced from the collection of Mr S. Peck.

The invaluable assistance provided by Mr Bernard Snell of the Fine Art Studio, Strood, Kent, in converting colour slides to black and white prints is gratefully acknowledged, as is the work done by B & D Computing of Highworth in converting computer data.

Thanks are due to the staff of the Swindon Fire Station, Swindon General Post Office, the AUEW Swindon office, and the Manager of the Wiltshire Hotel for their readiness to provide high level vantage points for photography.

Thanks are also due to the assistance and support of the Wilts and Berks Canal Amenity Group in the lead up to publication, greatly assisted by the facilities provided by Intergraph (UK) Ltd.

Finally, the advice and help given by Mr Jim Willis and Mr Terry Cave in printing and distribution are gratefully acknowledged.

**- oOo -**

Dedicated to the memory of
Jack Dalby

# CONTENTS

|  |  |  | Page |
|---|---|---|---|
| Introduction |  |  | 1 |
| Brief History |  |  | 2 |
| The Search for Information |  |  | 4 |
| Section I | - | Wilts and Berks Canal from the south western outskirts of Swindon to the former junction with the North Wilts branch. |  |
|  | - | History: 1794 - 1841 | 5 |
|  |  | 1841 - 1914 | 8 |
|  |  | 1914 to the present | 28 |
|  | - | Present Day Evidence of the Canal | 40 |
| Section II | - | Wilts and Berks Canal from the former junction with the North Wilts branch to the eastern outskirts of Swindon |  |
|  | - | History: 1794 - 1841 | 47 |
|  |  | 1841 - 1914 | 49 |
|  |  | 1914 to the present | 58 |
|  | - | Present Day Evidence of the Canal | 68 |
| Section III | - | North Wilts Canal from its junction with the Wilts and Berks Canal in Swindon to Moredon. |  |
|  | - | History: 1814 - 1841 | 75 |
|  |  | 1841 - 1914 | 76 |
|  |  | 1914 to the present | 89 |
|  | - | Present Day Evidence of the Canal | 98 |
|  |  | The Future | 105 |
| Table One | - | Bridges over the Wilts and Berks Canal and the North Wilts branch in the Swindon area 1803 - 1993. |  |
|  | - | Section I - Wilts and Berks Canal from the south western outskirts of Swindon to the former junction with the North Wilts branch | 106 |
|  | - | Section II - Wilts and Berks Canal from the former junction with the North Wilts branch to the eastern outskirts of Swindon | 111 |
|  | - | Section III - North Wilts Canal from its junction with the Wilts and Berks Canal in Swindon to Moredon | 116 |

Table Two     -     Summarised sequence of in filling of the Wilts and
                          Berks Canal and the North Wilts branch in the Swindon
                          area 1914 - 1993.                                                      123

List of References                                                                         127

List of Illustrations                                                                      132

## INTRODUCTION

The aim of this manuscript is to record the factual evidence relating to the Wilts and Berks Canal and its North Wilts branch in the town of Swindon. By coupling this compilation of facts with a photographic slide record of present day sites along the route of the canal, it is hoped to preserve at least some of the information on an important piece of 19th century industrial archaeology from total loss in the face of extensive re-development now taking place in Swindon.

It should be emphasized at the outset that the author did not commence research for this manuscript until 1971 and has no direct acquaintance with canal artefacts and remains which were destroyed prior to this date. All the pre-1971 information has been derived from research of documented information and the contributions received from numerous individuals.

The author would welcome supplementary information from readers with more direct acquaintance with the old canal prior to 1971.

The bulk of the work on this manuscript was completed in 1979, but was subsequently updated in 1985. Since 1985, several abortive attempts at publication have been made, finally ending in 1990 with Wiltshire County Council's intention to publish in their series of Local History Studies being frustrated by budgetary restrictions. That publication has at last been achieved is due to the enthusiasm of, and the resources provided by, the Wilts and Berks Canal Amenity Group, and the invaluable advice and assistance provided by Mr Jim Willis and Mr Terry Cave.

The continuing redevelopment of Swindon has meant that further changes to the environs of the old canal have occurred since 1985, and the manuscript has been updated to include these changes wherever possible.

**- oOo -**

# THE WILTS AND BERKS CANAL - A BRIEF HISTORY

The following brief history of the Wilts and Berks canal is quoted verbatim from an article by Mr Reg Wilkinson published in 1974[49]:

"The Wilts and Berks Canal was one of the three East-West canals constructed in the south of England during the years of "canal mania". The proprietors and William Whitworth, its engineer, intended it to become part of a national network of profitable manmade waterways which would provide a more reliable method of transport than the shallow rivers and the muddy turnpike roads.

The canal started from its junction with the Kennet and Avon Canal at Semington, and ran in a northerly direction between the Cotswold Hills and the Marlborough Downs, then on through the Vale of the White Horse to join the River Thames at Abingdon.

Constructed under an Act of 1796, the waterway had reached Swindon by 1804 and when completed, six years later, including branches to Chippenham, Calne, Longcot and Wantage, it had cost over £250,000. In 1819 the W&B was joined to the Thames and Severn Canal by the North Wilts Canal which ran from Swindon to Latton and cost an additional £35,000. The main line was 52 miles in length and the branches, including the North Wilts, added about 15 miles to the waterway.

## Coals and Cargoes

Coal was carried on the canal in an easterly direction and corn and agricultural products were collected from the wharves on the return journey for distribution in the cities of Bath and Bristol. The coal originated from the Somerset coalfield and reached the W&B via the Somerset Coal Canal and the K&A. Bath stone, timber, groceries and a variety of other goods were also carried on the waterway but 75% of the traffic was coal.

Financially, the W&B was never a tremendous success. Tolls increased slowly to reach a maximum of about £15,000 in 1837. Regular dividends were not paid to shareholders until the 1830s and they were reasonable for only about a decade. In the early years profits were used on general improvements or to repay the £13,000 borrowed from the Exchequer Loan Commissioners when funds ran out during the construction of the North Wilts.

In common with many other independent canals which ran through agricultural districts, the arrival of the railways brought financial ruin to the W&B. Railway lines which followed the routes of the W&B and the North Wilts were both completed in 1841.

Several different organisations tried to make the waterway pay after this but none were successful. In 1887 the owners applied for a Warrant of Abandonment, but this was not granted and the W&B struggled on until 1906 when all traffic ceased due to a burst at the western end. Swindon Corporation obtained an Act of Closure in 1914 and the W&B was officially abandoned."

A more detailed history of the canal is given in L J Dalby's book "The Wilts and Berks Canal"[1], which has proved an invaluable source of information during these investigations.

# THE SEARCH FOR INFORMATION

The material recorded in this manuscript has been obtained from many sources, principally the Swindon Reference Library, the Wiltshire County Records Office at Trowbridge, and the Archaeology Division of the Ordnance Survey, over the period 1971-1985. Even during this short period of time there have been changes in the old canal and its environs.

It is convenient to consider the three legs of the canal which met in the centre of Swindon (at the spot now occupied by the Primark stores in the Parade) separately as follows:

Section I: Wilts and Berks Canal from the south western outskirts of Swindon to the former junction with the North Wilts Branch (Grid Reference 137835 to 151849).

Section II: Wilts and Berks Canal from the former junction with the North Wilts Branch to the eastern outskirts of Swindon (Grid Reference 151849 to 185861).

Section III: North Wilts Canal from its junction with the Wilts and Berks Canal to Moredon (Grid Reference 151849 to 122873).

The route of the canal through Swindon is illustrated in Fig. 1, p. 6 by dotted lines on a 1945 street plan (taken from Reference 2).

Each Section will consist of two parts - history and present day evidence of the canal.

The historical part is subdivided into three in each case to relate to the most important dates in the canal's life, thus:-

1794-1841 covers the period from the initial survey (1794) to the arrival of the Great Western Railway (1841) - the canal's best years.

1841-1914 the period from the arrival of the railway to the Act of Abandonment (1914) - the years of decline.

1914 to the present - the period after abandonment.

A summarised description of the various bridges built over the canal in the Swindon area is given in Table 1 and a timetable of infilling in Table 2.

**SECTION ONE:
WILTS AND BERKS CANAL
FROM THE SOUTH WESTERN OUTSKIRTS OF SWINDON
TO THE FORMER JUNCTION WITH THE NORTH WILTS BRANCH
(GRID REFERENCES 137835 TO 151849).**

## HISTORY

Dalby's book[1] contains a diagram of the Wilts and Berks Canal and the North Wilts Branch. No locks are shown on the main canal within the section under consideration, the nearest being at Chaddington (near Wootton Bassett) in the west (GR092817) and at South Marston to the east (GR195868).

This summit section through Swindon was completed in 1805 and the canal was finally opened through to the Thames at Abingdon by September 10th, 1810[1].

The Wilts and Berks was a narrow canal, on the advice of Whitworth, and Dalby[1] has suggested that this recommendation was due to two factors:

a) Most of the trade was expected to come from barges using the Somerset Coal Canal, which was a narrow canal, and

b) The cost of a broad canal was estimated to be £336,000 compared to £289,000 for a narrow one.

The dimensions recommended by Whitworth were 27 ft at the surface, 14 ft at the bottom with a depth of 4.5 ft. In the event, the canal was eventually constructed to larger dimensions, and Harcourts "Rivers and Canals" quotes dimensions of 40 ft width at the surface, 20 ft wide at the bottom, with a depth of 4 ft in open country. Under bridges this reference quotes a narrowing to 12 ft width with a 6 ft wide towpath.

Dalby states that at summit level (ie, in the Swindon area) the canal was excavated 2 ft deeper and 6 ft wider than elsewhere to provide an adequate water supply to lower levels. Measurements taken from large scale Ordnance Survey maps and from local council plans give canal widths ranging between 32 and 40 ft, depending on location. Initially, water supply for the summit level was provided by feeders from Wroughton Brook (from Deacon's Mill, West Leaze) and from Wanborough Brook[1].

### 1794-1841

An undated hand drawn map 20 inches to the mile of the Wilts and Berks Canal is held in Swindon Reference Library. Dalby[9] suspects that this map was a construction map drawn for Robert Whitworth, surveyor of the canal, as part of the survey report of 1794. A similar map of the North Wilts Branch, also held in the Swindon Reference Library, was drawn by William McIlquham.

This, the earliest map of the canal, showed five bridges on this section, on at GR138838, about a quarter of a mile south west of Kingshill Road, another 200 yds south west of

Fig. 1: Swindon Street Plan c 1945 (Victoria County History of Wiltshire)

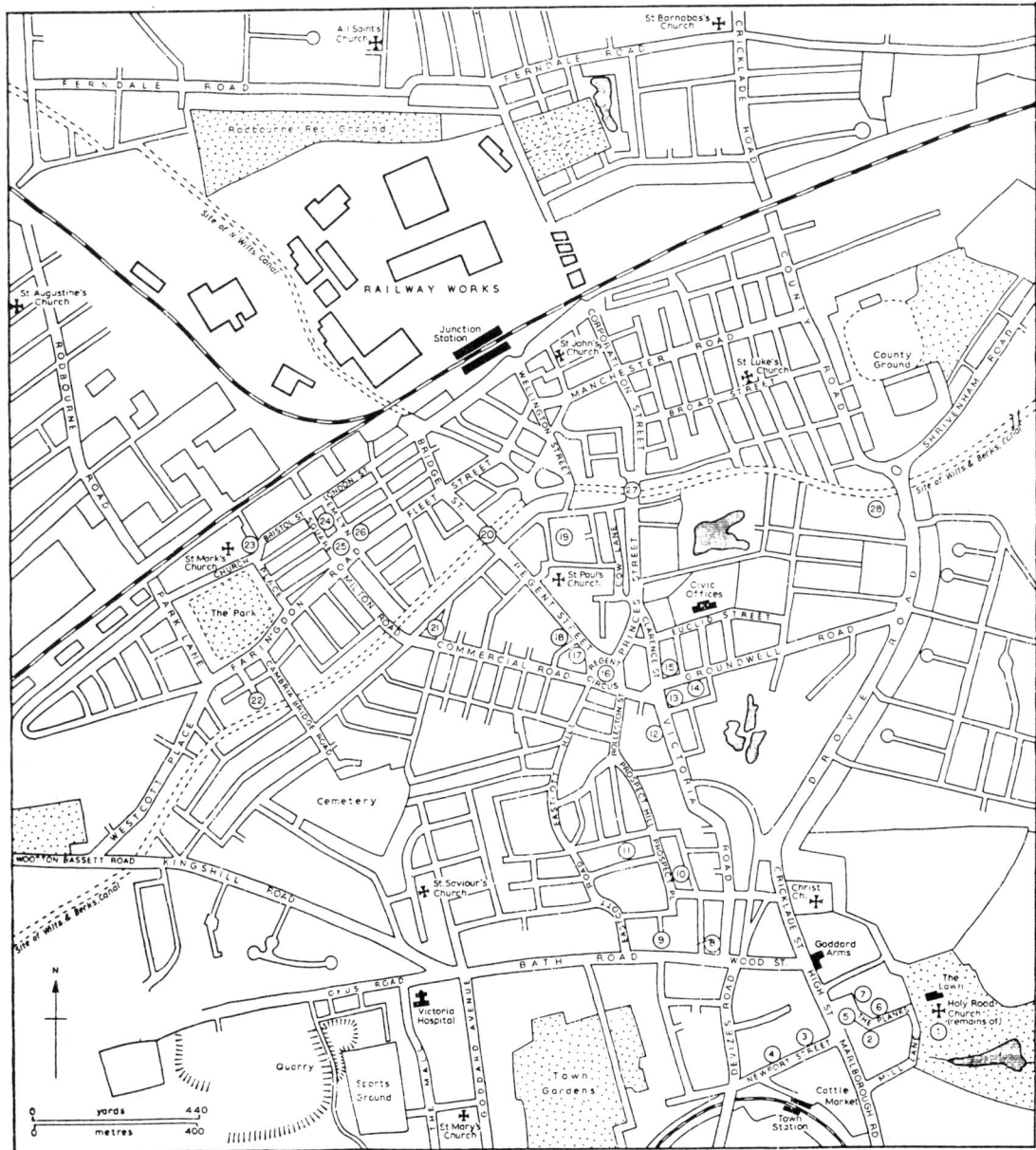

Kingshill Road, then Kingshill Road (GR141840), "Black" Bridge (GR147845) and "Golden Lion" Bridge (GR150848), although the bridges were not known by these names at the time. If the map is indeed the survey map of 1794, then clearly this pre-dates the construction of the canal (1805) and the showing of the bridges indicates an intention to construct only. This is exemplified by the fact that the bridge shown 200 yds south west of Kingshill Road did not appear on any maps produced after completion of the canal, and was probably never built. The remaining four bridges were shown on the 1818 two inches to the mile drawing No 166, a copy of which is held by the Archaeology Division of the Ordnance Survey at Southampton. These drawings formed the basis of the first edition of the famous Ordnance Survey one inch to the mile maps, and the map covering this part of the canal was issued for the first time in 1820, the detail corresponding to that on the two inch drawing.

It is fairly certain from both the Wilts and Berks Works Ledgers (held by Swindon Reference Library) and later maps that Kingshill Road Bridge, a stone arch bridge, was built in 1804 or possibly slightly earlier (1803). The bridge at GR138838 is referred to in Wilts and Berks Works Ledger A of 1803 - "building a drawbridge near Okus (Oakhouse) on Mr Goddard's land"[10]. The dates of construction of the other bridges, which were probably wooden swing or draw bridges, are less certain, but were almost certain contemporary with Kingshill Road Bridge.

The 1820 Ordnance Survey map shows that tracks from settlements at South Leaze and West Leaze converged about a quarter of a mile south west of the Okus bridge and continued on to meet the canal towpath at the western end of the bridge. Thereafter the track ran parallel to the towpath to Kingshill Road, thereby providing the shortest feasible access to Old Town from the two settlements. In all probability the alternative route over the bridge to Okus and up the hill was beyond the capabilities of horse drawn carts and wagons due to the severity of the gradient, but it would have been feasible for pack horses and foot traffic.

Kingshill Road Bridge, known at the time as Rushey Platt Bridge, was mentioned in Wilts and Berks Works Ledger A of 1803, and again in Works Ledger B (1804)[10]. The latter stated that the Canal Company was obliged to provide solidly constructed bridges on the Wootton Bassett Road, Cricklade Road and Lower Eastcott Farm Road. The first two bridges were Kingshill Road and Drove Road bridges and both roads were turnpikes. The identity of the third bridge is by no means certain, since reference to two different Eastcott bridges was made in Works Ledger B of 1804. One almost certainly "Whale" Bridge, whilst the other was either "Black" Bridge or the "Golden Lion" Bridge.

Works Ledger B (1804) refers to a wooden swing bridge to carry the bridleway from Eastcott to Rodbourne Cheney, whereas another entry dated 1806 states "Carpenter making drawbridges at road at Eastcott, Marsh Farm, etc"[10]. It is possible that the first reference is to "Black" Bridge and the second to "Golden Lion" Bridge.

The confusion relating to the two Eastcotts is due to the fact that in the case of Black Bridge and the Golden Lion Bridge, the reference to Eastcott almost certainly related to the nearby settlement of Eastcott south of the canal under the hill from Old Town, whereas in the case of Whale Bridge, the reference probably related to Lower Eastcott Farm which was situated some distance away from the other Eastcott, to the north of the canal, on a site where the Thamesdown bus depot is today.

About half a mile south west of Kingshill Road Bridge the canal crossed the River Ray over a stone aqueduct, which had two sturdy arches through which the river flowed. This aqueduct still exists today.

An 1810 map of Wiltshire[11], held by Swindon Reference Library, shows bridges over the canal at Rushey Platt and Cricklade Road (Drove Road) but none between, in contrast to the 1820 first edition of the Ordnance Survey one inch to the mile map referred to earlier, which shows additional bridges in positions corresponding to "Black" Bridge and "Golden Lion" Bridge; "Black" Bridge is also shown on an 1826 map published in Reference 8. This inconsistency throws doubt upon the standard of revision of the 1810 map, which was based on an earlier edition of 1773.

A statement in Works Ledger A[10], referring to the smaller wooden bridges on the canal, says that for the first two years of canal construction (1795-1797) swivel bridges were built; later only drawbridges (other than fixed bridges) were built. Since the canal construction did not reach the Swindon area until 1803/1804, this should imply that all minor bridges in this area were drawbridges, but clearly this policy was not applied rigorously, since, as mentioned earlier, Works Ledger B (1804) refers to a swing bridge ("Black" Bridge) to carry the bridleway from Eastcott to Rodbourne Cheney.

Joseph Priestley was appointed as the canal's first manager in 1810, but he only stayed seven years, to be succeeded in 1817 by William Dunsford, who remained Manager until his death in 1845.

No building development took place in the vicinity of the canal during this period.

## 1841-1914

If the previous period marked the best years of the Wilts and Berks canal, the period 1841-1914 represented its gradual decline and final death. The prime agent in this was the arrival of the Great Western Railway which gave birth to New Swindon but killed the canal by draining its lifeblood - trade.

The line to Bristol was opened on 30th June 1841, crossing the North Wilts Branch of the canal just north of its junction with the main canal. The railway works opened in 1843 and underwent continuous enlargement from that date up to and beyond the turn of the century[2]. The station was opened in July 1842, the same year that building of the railway cottages started[2]. On the death of William Dunsford in 1845, his son took over as Canal Manager.

Between 1845 and 1850 the houses of Westcott Place and Westcott Street were built on the west bank of the canal just to the north of Rushey Platt (Kingshill Road) bridge[2]. The buildings of Westcott Place were similar in architecture to Cetus Buildings, which were also built in the 1840s (see Section II).

These houses, and Cetus Buildings, are thought to have been built by the Canal Company for their employees, and the terrace included "The Falcon", a public house which is still in use today. A rear entrance to "The Falcon" gave direct access from the canal tow-path.

A recent publication[99] detailing the history of public houses in North Wiltshire provides further information regarding the building of Westcott Place. There were four pubs in Westcott Place during the 1840/1850s. In order from the Wootton Bassett Road end they were the Wild Deer (62 Westcott Place), the Greyhound (rear of 46 Westcott Place), the Duke of York (no. 43) and the Falcon (no. 40). With the exception of the Greyhound, now demolished, all these buildings still exist, with the Duke of York now a private house, but both the Wild Deer and the Falcon are still pubs.

The Wild Deer was built in 1847 by Charles Hedges, a baker. The Greyhound was a canal side pub which was once (or was next door to) the Canal Company's blacksmith shop. It must have opened some time after 1830 as a beer house and closed in 1859, its trade no doubt taken away by the Falcon, Duke of York and Wild Deer, all within 100 yards or so[99]. It was let in 1859 as a private house.

The Duke of York was the end building in Falcon Terrace which was built by the Canal Company. It was only in use as a beer house from 1851 to 1856 after which it seems to have been an Off Licence[99].

The Falcon, from which the terrace got its name, was built c. 1849. The earliest letting was in 1849-1850.

The Canal Company also owned the Whale, next to the Whale Bridge and the Old Locomotive and Wholesome Barrel on the North Wilts[99]. (See Sections II and III.)

Two paintings of "New Swindon" in 1849, showing the new Railway Works and the Railway Village, are on display in Swindon. They are very similar in viewpoint, style and size, but differ slightly in detail, and both provide much useful information on the canal and its environs. The painting in the Railway Museum is entitled "New Swindon in 1849" and was presented by the sons of I K Brunel. The view is from the west, looking east along the railway towards the "Railway Village" and Swindon Station. Parts of the main canal and the North Wilts Branch are shown. Apart from the buildings of the Railway Village and in the vicinity of the station, very little development is visible, most of the scene being fields. Some development has occurred in the vicinity of the Golden Lion Bridge, which, in this painting, effectively hides the bridge from view. Barges are shown on the canal. A photograph of this painting is shown in Fig. 2.

The other painting is in Swindon Museum in Old Town, and the slightly different viewpoint permits the Golden Lion Bridge to be seen. Even on the quite large original watercolour, it needs a magnifying glass to bring out the fact that a flat span drawbridge, with lifting gear on the southern bank, is depicted at the Golden Lion location.

An 1850 map of Swindon shown in the Swindon Borough Council publication "Studies in the History of Swindon"[8] shows Kingshill Road Bridge, Black Bridge and the Golden Lion Bridge.

By 1849 the Golden Lion public house (built by James Edwards, a coal merchant) was in use[99] and it was this pub that gave the bridge its name. The Golden Lion itself was a life-size effigy of a lion mounted on the roof of the pub and can be seen in a 1918 photograph (converted to a transparency) held by Swindon Museum[21]. The origins of the name Black Bridge are obscure, but it has been suggested[10] that the bridge might have been tarred in the same way that early swivel bridges on the Berkeley and Gloucester canal were treated with tar at road level.

An 1850 map of Swindon reproduced in the form of a transparency is included in a large collection of slides held by Swindon Museum[21]. Bridges shown on this section of the canal are those at Rushey Platt (Okus), Kingshill Road, Black Bridge, but rather surprisingly no bridge is shown at the Golden Lion, although the tracks leading to the canal (later Bridge Street/Regent Street) are shown.

During the period 1851-61 the most important development in New Swindon was the building of houses "along the lane from Eastcott to the end of Fleetway, and so north to the Union Railway Inn"[2]. This is now the line of Regent and Bridge Streets and crossed the canal at the Golden Lion Bridge. By 1861 the part south of the canal contained some 50 houses with about the same number north of the canal in Waterloo Terrace, Bellwood Place, Alma Terrace and Albion Terrace, all of which were demolished during redevelopment in the 1960s. According to the Victoria County History of Wiltshire (Vol IX)[2], this growth of the Bridge Street area was sporadic and confined to what were only workmen's cottages and beerhouses. "The street contained only four small shops and ran from a farmyard at the Eastcott (southern) end past a brick field and waste ground near the canal."

F Large in his book "Swindon in Retrospect 1856-1931"[7] mentions Black Bridge in a chapter titled "Schoolday Recollections", and since he was born in 1852, this reference can be dated as some time in the late 1850s.

A transparency in the Swindon Museum collection[21] shows a view of Swindon New Town in 1860, the photograph being a panoramic view from south of the canal looking towards the Railway Works, the Park and St Marks Church. No bridges are visible in the photograph, the length of canal in view being too far east of Kingshill Road and too far west of Black Bridge for these to be seen. The canal passes through fields and is fenced along the south bank for the whole length in view. The north bank, which was embanked above the lower ground to the north, has a line of bushes along the edge of the towpath. The view would have included the site of the Cambria Bridge.

Between 1861 and 1871 the population of New Swindon increased by 83% to 7,628[2]. Continued development of the Westcott Place area near to Kingshill Road Bridge took place during this period, to provide accommodation for the influx of labour induced by the rapid expansion of the Railway Works. Rolling mills were built in 1861, and in 1869 the carriage works opened. Many Welsh families moved to the town to work in the rolling mills, and for their accommodation the stone fronted terraces of Cambria Place (GR144844) were built in 1862[2].

A year earlier, the works of the New Swindon Gas Company had been established on the north bank of the canal just to the west of the Golden Lion Bridge, in Queen Street (GR148847)[2]. This site was cleared for redevelopment in August 1973.

In 1867 that part of Bridge Street south of the canal was renamed Regent Street. Richard Jeffries had some caustic comments to make on the state of the Golden Lion Bridge in 1967 in his book "Jeffriesland - a History of Swindon"[13]. In a chapter headed "Swindon in 1867" he says "This Bridge Street, now so much used, was formerly a mere track made by waggon wheels across furrows, which crossed the canal at the Golden Lion Bridge. That bridge, by the by, is a disgrace to the town." Replacement of the old wooden drawbridge had in fact been advocated as early as 1854[2] to meet the demands of the greatly increased traffic of workmen journeying to the Railway Works. The old bridge was eventually replaced with an iron lift bridge built by the Great Western Railway Company in 1870[1]. The bridge had a central span which was lifted vertically by chains acting in hollow pillars positioned at the ends of the span[10]. Details of the operating mechanism, which utilised a capstan sited at the Regent Street end of the bridge to drive the chain pulleys through a system of bevel gears and drive rods, are illustrated in a series of drawings prepared for the

Swindon New Town Local Board in December 1869 and January 1870. These and several other very informative bridge plans prepared for the Town Council are held in the Wiltshire County Records Office at Trowbridge[51]. Below the hollow pillars were 10 feet deep chambers in which the counterweights moved.

Another set of plans, undated but obviously contemporary, show an alternative design for the bridge, rather more ornate but operating on the same principle. Presumably the New Town Board decided against this proposal in favour of the one described in the previous paragraph. The rejected plans are stamped "T.E.M. Marsh, Bath". Although Dalby states that the favoured design was built by the Great Western Railway Company[1], there is nothing on the plans themselves to indicate that the GWR were in any way involved, although clearly the work would have been well suited to their manufacturing facilities.

In 1871 a terrace of 15 houses (which has since disappeared in redevelopment) was built on a narrow strip of ground between King Street (GR 149848) and the canal[2], and in 1873 a school was built in College Street on the east bank of the canal just south of the junction with the North Wilts Canal. The canal ran immediately behind College Street School and proved later to be a great hazard for the children[2]. The school was originally built by the GWR but was handed over to the Swindon School Board in the 1880s for a nominal rental[63].

Extensions were made to the Golden Lion public house in 1875[99].

1877 saw the construction of a new bridge over the canal in the Welsh part of the town, near to Cambria Place at GR 145844. This bridge was called Cambria Bridge, and it still exists today (in modified form). It is now a flat span reinforced concrete road bridge with brick abutments and parapets, the latter surmounted by steel railings. According to Dalby[1], James Hinton paid £200 to the Canal Company for the right to construct the original bridge over the canal. Hinton was a speculative builder and a former Mayor of Swindon[52]. Evidence from Swindon New Town Local Board plans[51] and copies of the legal documents relating to the bridge held in Swindon Library[53] indicates that the original bridge was a steel girder span of 22 ft between brick abutments. Steel side rails between wooden posts lined the approaches and main span, the approaches being embanked on both sides of the canal and rising to 8 ft above canal level at the bridge itself.

The agreement with Hinton[53], Document C168, dated 7th May 1877, makes interesting reading:

> "The purchaser will commence on Monday, 21st May next to erect ...... a bridge ...... 8 ft high above water level when the canal is full to the lower side of the girders upon which the bridge shall be supported ...... clear waterway 12 ft wide ...... towpath 6 ft wide ...... foundations to be completed by 4th June. No obstruction of the canal after this date ...... completely finish work on bridge supports within 2 months of 21st May."

The conveyance to Hinton, Document C169[53], is dated 3rd December 1877. This shows the width of the bridge cross-section to be 20 ft. (In practice the overall width turned out to be 22 ft[51].)

Fig. 2: New Swindon, 1849   (Swindon Museum Collection)

Fig. 3: Black Bridge and the Railway Village, 1885 (Swindon Museum Collection)

The inadequacy of the canal bridges in the face of Swindon's rapidly increasing population was causing great inconvenience, and even the relatively new Golden Lion Bridge frequently made men late for work (at the Railway Works) when it was up[2]. In 1877 a fixed footbridge of the type used on the railways (with a raised central span reached by steps on either side) was placed beside it by public subscription[2].

Between 1877 and 1880 some 300 houses were built forming the eastern part of Albion and William Streets, just south of Cambria Bridge on the east bank of the canal[2]. About this time, a timber yard was established by Messrs Webbs at the northern end of Albion Street adjacent to the bridge. A warehouse was built on what is now the site of Day's Garage (and was demolished when the garage was built) (Fig. 4). The wharf was known as Cambria Bridge Wharf. A photograph taken at this time (apparently from Cambria Bridge) is shown in Fig. 5 and beyond the timber yard can be seen the developed eastern side of Albion Street. These houses still exist today, and particular note should be taken of the shop on the extreme left. This is now a private house, but a tablet level with the upstairs windows records the date of construction as 1878.

A printed map of Swindon dated 1882 is held in Swindon Museum and shows both Cambria Bridge and Black Bridge (Fig. 6). The latter is shown connecting gardens on the north bank of the canal with fields on the south bank. The Golden Lion Bridge is also shown.

In 1883 the Swindon, Marlborough and Andover Railway (formed in 1881) extended their line to Cirencester, and the elegant brick arch bridge carrying the railway over the canal at GR 137835, which still stands today, was built (Fig. 7)[54]. The company adopted the name Midland and South Western Junction Railway in 1884.

Between 1873 and 1885 surveying of the Swindon area by the Ordnance Survey took place, leading to the production of the First Edition (1886) of the 1/2500 (25.344 inches/mile) large scale maps, the 1885/1886 10.56 ft to the mile plans of New Swindon and the 1889 six inches to the mile map of Swindon. Some of the larger scale maps are held in Swindon Reference Library, but the six inch map and the complete series of the large scale maps are held by the Ordnance Survey Headquarters at Southampton.

These maps provide an invaluable source of information on the canal and its environs during the latter part of the 19th century.

Sheet XV.7 of the 1/2500 series (surveyed 1883/4) shows the M and SWJ railway bridge and the canal bridge at Rushey Platt, Kingshill Road Bridge and Cambria Bridge with development in the Westcott Place/Cambria Place area on the west bank of the canal, and the northern ends of Albion Street and William Street on the east bank. By this time the western side of Albion Street had been developed, apart from a space corresponding to the position of Webb's timber yard. The larger scale 10.56 ft/mile plans show that Kingshill Road Bridge was a masonry arch bridge, whilst Cambria Bridge corresponds to the configuration described earlier (the James Hinton Bridge).

Fig. 4: Webb's Timber Yard and Warehouse, Cambria Bridge Wharf 1880s

The canal bridge at Rushey Platt (GR138838) is outside the coverage of the 10.56 ft/mile plans (as is the railway bridge) but the 1/2500 map shows that the central span has been removed since 1804, although the abutments remain. The reason for this change must remain a mystery in the absence of any information.

To the north east of Cambria Bridge there was a large undeveloped area until the Bridge Street/Regent Street development was reached. This area was the Rollestone Estate on which legal restrictions prevented development until 1885[2]. Sheet XV8 of the 1/2500 series (surveyed 1885) covers this area, and shows Black Bridge carrying a track from farm buildings set in fields on the south east of the canal towards Faringdon Road to the north of the canal. An 1885 photograph exhibited in the "Farewell Swindon Borough" exhibition held in 1974[14] showed a panorama of the Railway Village and Works from a viewpoint east of the canal. In the foreground are the fields and farm mentioned earlier, and the track leading to Black Bridge, which has raised approaches to a flat span with a gate at its eastern end. The photograph, which is reproduced in Fig. 3, p. 13, is rather indistinct, but the bridge appears to be of wooden construction, with wooden side railings, set upon brick or stone abutments. The caption to the photograph reads "In No 2 (the number of the photograph on display) there are the beginnings of a road opening off Faringdon Road opposite Emlyn Square, just where Milton Road begins today. It does not, however, follow the line of Milton Road, but cuts across the future site of the Baths building to a canal bridge, known as Black Bridge, sited some distance west of the present Milton Road Bridge. The main purpose seems to have been farm access."

Fig. 5: Cambria Bridge Wharf 1880s

Fig. 7: Rushey Platt Railway Bridge, June 1991

Fig. 6: 1882 Map of Swindon by Orlando Baker (Swindon Museum Collection)

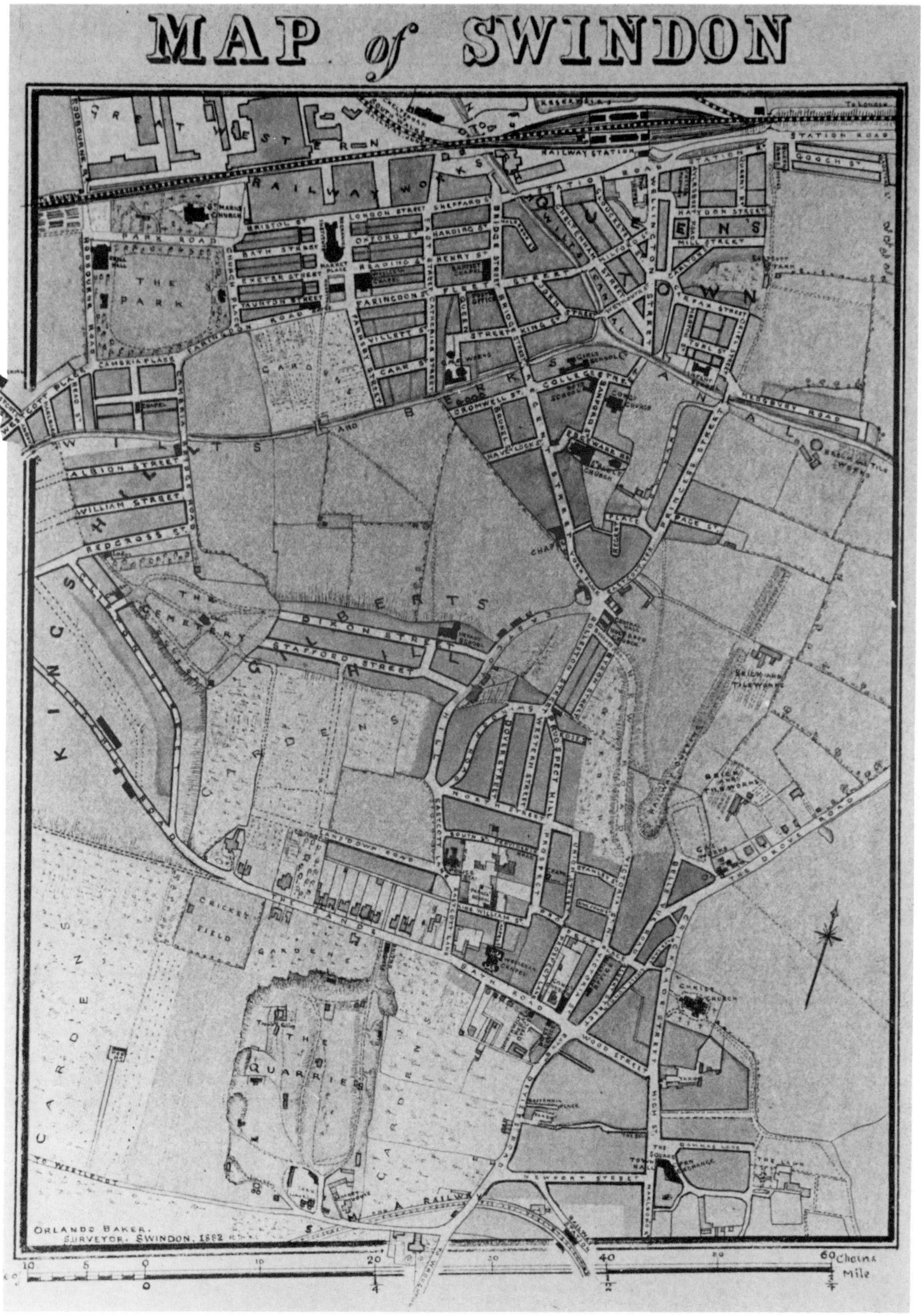

Another photograph of Black Bridge is held by the Swindon Local History Society[55]. Although undated it appears to be of similar vintage (1885) to the photograph shown in the "Farewell Swindon Borough" exhibition, and is taken from a similar but slightly lower viewpoint, demonstrating even more conclusively that by this time Black Bridge was a fixed bridge with embanked approaches. Works Ledger B in 1804 referred to the original bridge as a swing bridge, so at some stage between 1804 and 1885 Black Bridge must have been converted to a fixed bridge. The Swindon Local History Society have enlarged the portion of the photograph containing the bridge, and this provides detailed information on its construction. Brick or masonry abutments carry the bridge span high above the canal, the span itself being a flat platform of wood or steel with posts and horizontal rails on each side.

The gate at the eastern (farm) end is a substantial one, being clad overall with vertical wooden planks. The 1885 1/2500 OS map shows embanked approaches at right angles to the canal, but in the photograph the embankment on the western approach appears to have been cut through to allow a track from the towpath to run into the open ground of the Rollestone Estate. This open ground appears to be already marked out in readiness for the forthcoming development subsequent to the lifting of the legal restrictions in 1885. It is not possible to see whether alternative access to the bridge was provided by the developers.

Sheet XV421 of the 10.56 ft/mile plans (surveyed 1885) shows the centre of New Swindon, with the Golden Lion Bridge (named as such) and the Golden Lion Hotel at its NW corner. A small footbridge is shown on the NE side of the main bridge - presumably the 1877 one. The 1/2500 map of the same area (Sheet XV4) designates College Street School as "School (Girls)". (See Fig. 28, Page 84.)

The Victoria County History[2] states that in 1885 the south western end of Albion Street and William Street, marked out in 1880, still had no houses on them, and this is confirmed by the maps just described.

Many paintings of the period, usually undated, but the majority of which are thought to have been executed about 1888-1890[10], are held in Swindon Museum. These paintings are part of a collection presented to the Swindon Public Library by Councillor Powell in 1907. An associated catalogue of these paintings and engravings dated 1907 is thought to be held by the Public Library. According to Tapscott-Mason[52], the Swindon Town Guides for 1934 and 1936 stated that the paintings held by the Museum formed a very small part of the total collection. Many others were placed in various secondary and other schools. The artist's name is thought to have been Puckey. Two of these show Kingshill Road Bridge, with the canal in a weedy condition. One is a view from the north entitled "Claredon Cottages, Kingshill". The bridge is shown as a stone arch bridge, with the cottages adjacent to its eastern end, on the northern side of Kingshill Road. The cottages still exist today, but have been subjected to considerable alteration in the intervening period. Kingshill itself appears in the background of the painting.

Another painting entitled "Old Golden Lion Bridge" shows the bridge in its post-1877 configuration, that is with raised footbridges alongside the main span. The hollow pillars containing the lifting chains are shown at each corner, with iron lattice work railings along either side of the lifting span. Two raised footbridges, one on each side, are shown, again with iron lattice work railings. Reference 2 mentions only one footbridge as being constructed in 1877, so it must be assumed that a second footbridge was added at a later date.

A transparency copied from an 1885 photograph, held by Swindon Museum, shows only one footbridge[21], so it seems likely that the second footbridge was added after 1885. A similar photograph is reproduced in Peter Sheldon's book "Swindon in Camera"[60]. Further confirmation is provided by the 1886 1/2500 OS map referred to earlier, which was surveyed in 1885 and shows only one footbridge.

The canal was by this time in financial difficulties following loss of trade to the Great Western Railway, and the working out of the Somerset coalfield which provided a major proportion of its cargo. Moves for abandonment were taken as early as 1874, but were defeated by sale of the canal to new owners - The Wilts and Berks Canal Company - in 1877. (The first owners were the Wilts and Berks Canal Navigation.) In 1874 it was reported that it had taken ten days to get a load to Wantage and three boats to do it, the depth of water being so little and the locks and bridges so out of repair[1]. The hand drawn map of the North Wilts Branch held by Swindon Reference Library, drawn by William McIlquham in 1820, was clearly used in the conveyance of the canal to the new owners, since it is annotated "Conveyance from the Wilts and Berks Canal Navigation to the Wilts and Berks Canal Company, 15th March 1877". It is further annotated alongside the various bridges and locks shown with comments on their state of repair (or lack of it). The purchase price was £13,496 and many sections of earlier Acts relating to the canal were repealed[1]. The canal was at all times to be kept open and navigable. Swindon New Town was given powers to erect bridges, while gas and water companies could lay mains across the canal.

The new Company spent over £17,000 on repairs but all to no avail. By 1882 tolls had fallen to £800, and the canal was then leased to a Bristol group who did their utmost to foster and stimulate trade on the canal by putting as much as possible of their own traffic on it[1]. By 1888 the Bristol Group had lost £16,000 and gave up their lease paying a forfeit of £1,000. The Wilts and Berks Canal Company resumed management[1]. In April of that year the only published account of a pleasure trip on the Wilts and Berks Canal appeared in Pall Mall Magazine[15]. The trip along the 54 miles of the Wilts and Berks, from Semington to Abingdon, through 42 locks, took five days. Quoting directly from the article; "The owner of a houseboat on the Kennet and Avon Canal, who had very kindly offered us the use of his craft on this water, wrote 'Nothing but a common trade boat will, at present, go up the Wilts and Berks Canal, as the bridges (wooden) are too low, and out of order; unless these were properly kept it would not be worthwhile making a boat to suit them'. However, this did not deter the intrepid explorers, and their comments on the offending bridges were '... there are a good many swing bridges on the Kennet and Avon and (much more troublesome) lift bridges on the Wilts canal ... those on the Kennet and Avon swing open on a pivot, as a rule; those on the Wilts and Berks lift vertically, with balance weights ...'".

In 1888, the Wilts and Berks carried 33,000 tons and collected £843 in tolls[1]. In 1891, the charge made to the GWR for taking water from the North Wilts branch was increased from £250 to £300 per annum, and in the same year another new group, the United Commercial Syndicate, took over the canal[1]. Under their manager, W J Ainsworth, the new Company spent £16,000 on dredging and lock repairs, putting the canal in substantially efficient working order from Semington to Swindon. They formed a separate carrying organisation and operated a series of twelve regular fast boats.

Fig. 8: Milton Road Bridge, February 1972

With the end of the legal restrictions which had prevented development until 1885, rapid development of the Rollestone Estate occurred between 1885 and 1901, connecting the earlier developments at Kingshill Road/Cambria Bridge in the west to New Swindon in the east[2]. The new development consisted of closely built brick terraces with Commercial Road as the axis of the whole scheme[2]. In the course of this development, Commercial Road Bridge, more commonly known as Milton Road Bridge, was built by Swindon Corporation in 1890[7], some 60 yds to the north east of Black Bridge (GR147845), which was probably removed around this time since the farm which it had served had been demolished during the development of the Rollestone Estate. Swindon New Town Local Board plans of Commercial Road Bridge, held by the County Records Office[51], are dated 25th September 1885, presumably prepared during negotiations for the development of the Rollestone Estate. In fact the title of the plans is "Rollestone Estate, Swindon. Bridge over Wilts and Berks Canal". Black Bridge is also shown on a location sketch which forms part of the plans, together with the preliminary layout (street ends only) of the proposed development between Cambria Bridge and Commercial Road. It is interesting to note that at the time this sketch was drawn Commercial Road was labelled "New Road" and Curtis Street was marked as an extension to Cromwell Street.

At the proposed site for the bridge, the canal was to be narrowed to 12 ft width (from 38 ft) by the construction of a 26 ft abutment projecting from the eastern bank. Embanked approaches on both sides of the bridge rose to 14 ft above the surrounding land at the bridge itself. This bridge, the most imposing canal bridge constructed in the Borough, is of brick construction, and still exists today, albeit modified by "renovation" in April 1981. The bridge in its original form is shown in Fig. 8, taken in February 1972. Note the elegant Bath stone balustrades. The 1885 plans of the bridge show each of the four corners of the balustrades as having wrought iron gas lamp standards on them. Three of the four columns were still there at the time of renovation in 1981, but the lamps had gone from the tops of the columns by then.

Also shown on the plans are side walls for steps or slopes coming down to canal level from each of the four corners of the bridge at the ends of the balustrades. These side walls are of brick with Bath stone coping stones surmounted by iron railings, and are still to be found today on the south west side of the bridge. (The steps and side wall on the north east side of the bridge at the Milton Road end were reconstructed in 1977.) What the plans do not show is the steps or slopes associated with these side walls, and therein lies a mystery. There were steps down to the towing path on both sides of the bridge at the north western (Milton Road) end between the wars[82], and yet these are not shown on the 1/2500 OS maps of 1900, 1923 and 1942. Whilst the steps had possibly been removed by the last date (1942) it would be expected that they would appear on the 1900 and 1923 maps, but even the side railings are not shown on these two maps (even though they must have been there) and first appear on the 1942 map. Another source [100], after consultation with local residents states that only one set of steps existed at the Milton Road end of the bridge, not two as described by Reference 82. These steps were on the north east side of the bridge, where the 1977 steps are now.

The question that remains unanswered is whether this was an omission by the Ordnance Survey, or were the steps not erected until after 1922 (the date of the revision of the 1923 map) and then removed before the 1942 map was surveyed (1942)? A painting by Puckey held in Swindon Museum does not help to solve the mystery. It shows the bridge viewed from the south western side, and must have been painted very early in the life of the bridge (1890 or thereabouts) since no buildings are to be seen (the Central Club, built 1897, would certainly have been in the field of view). The north west bank of the canal has a grassy bank alongside the towpath, and bushes on this bank hide the possible location of steps from view. On the opposite bank, the long abutment sticks well out into the canal, and a timber baulk runs from the bridge arch to the foot of the side wall running down to the canal level from the south eastern end of the bridge (Commercial Road end). This baulk is shown on the 1885 plans as being "12 in x 12 in pitch pine guides". The steel rails are shown on the side wall, but only run halfway down the coping stones. Inside the wall there is no slope, only rough ground at canal bank level. The top of the side wall is fenced off by a solid plank fence from Commercial Road. Whether the painting represents the bridge during the course of construction and therefore unfinished, or whether the side walls and their steel railings shown on the 1885 plans were meant to be purely ornamental features it is not possible to say without further information. The latter interpretation seems extremely unlikely in view of the fact that steps and slopes were later constructed inside these side walls. Measurements of the gradients of the railings on the original plans match those found on the site today on the south western side of the bridge. As stated earlier, it can therefore be assumed that they date from the original construction in 1890. At 1 in 2 the gradient of the railings at the Milton Road end of the bridge is considerably steeper than those at the Commercial Road end at 1 in 3.3. The steeper gradient corresponds with steps (it is the same as that of the 1977 reconstructed steps on the north eastern corner of the bridge) whilst the shallower gradient probably corresponds with a slope.

Summarising then, it appears that steps were constructed down to the towpath at the Milton Road end of the bridge, and slopes down to the canal bank at the Commercial Road end of the bridge, but whether these features were part of the original construction or were added later is an unsolved question. A wharf was created on the north eastern side of the bridge, presumably to serve Swindon Market which was immediately adjacent to it on the other side of Wharf Road. The Market was built in 1892[2] and the nearby Central Club, fronting Milton Road on the north east side of the bridge, was built in 1897. The entrance to the Club was directly on the line of the slope down to the canal bank from the north eastern corner of the bridge, and if the slope was there in 1897, it would have necessarily been greatly altered during the building of the Club entrance. A photograph taken during the construction of the Central Club and converted into a transparency by Eric Arman is held by Swindon Museum[21]. It shows that the canal was dammed locally and drained whilst the foundations of the building were being laid. An undated water colour of Milton Road Bridge by A V Aubrey was exhibited at the "Farewell Swindon Borough" exhibition in 1974[14]. Unfortunately the author has been unable to trace this painting for further examination to see if it throws any light on the questions relating to the steps and slopes leading down to canal level. The Market was built by Swindon Corporation at a cost of £4,500 and was covered in 1903[22]. During this period (1885-1899) Webb's timber yard moved to a new site near to Bullens Bridge on the North Wilts canal, enabling development of the western side of Albion Street to be completed.

It appears that in spite of the addition of the raised footbridge in 1877 the Golden Lion Bridge was still proving a problem to the Swindon New Town Local Board in 1892. Plans held by the County Record Office[51], dated August 1892, show sketch plans for conversion to a fixed bridge, with canal traffic being accommodated by lowering the bed of the canal over a narrowed section under the bridge 200 ft long. The depth of water in this section was to be controlled by sluice gates at each end, the bed of the canal being 11.5 ft below the bottom of the bridge. When no barges were passing the gates were to be left open and the water depth was 10 ft. When barges wished to pass under the bridge, the gates were closed, and the water level lowered to 3.5 ft above the canal bed. This proposal was not proceeded with. Whether the second raised footbridge was already in position by this date, or whether it was added later (as a less effective but much cheaper solution to the traffic problem) is not known.

Fig. 9: Cambria Bridge, November 1975 (Built 1893)

The Golden Lion Bridge was not the only one to cause traffic problems in the rapidly growing town. Hinton's Cambria Bridge was also proving inadequate, and plans for widening this bridge and its approaches, one of which is dated 9th November 1892, are held in the County Record Office[51]. In contrast to the Golden Lion proposals, the local board adopted the Cambria Bridge proposals and the bridge was widened in 1893 at a cost of £1,500[56]. The bridge had its width increased from the 22 ft of the Hinton bridge to 34 ft with the approaches being widened to match. Foundations to the towpath and the abutments were strengthened, with 2 ft of extra brickwork being added to the abutments beneath the ends of the span. The span itself was also strengthened by the substitution of load carrying sheet steel sides for the non-load carrying posts and railings on the earlier bridge. The steel sides were built into brick end pillars and contained six riveted panels a side, additionally supported by two external stiffening sections equidistant from the ends of the span. Details of the original Hinton bridge are also shown on these plans. Cambria Bridge, which must still be fresh in the memory of many Swindonians since it stood unaltered until May 1978, seemed to be the model which the Swindon New Town Local Board adopted for several of its bridges, since Queenstown Bridge (1885) and the rebuilt Whale Bridge (1893) were of similar design (see Section II). The more grandiose Milton Road Bridge was an exception, possibly due to the need to meet the wishes of the owners of the Rollestone estate. The pre-1978 version of Cambria Bridge is shown in Fig. 9.

In the meantime, the United Commercial Syndicate were not faring too well as new owners of the canal. In spite of their intensive restoration efforts in 1891, tolls over the next three years averaged only £600 and by 1894 the canal had silted up to a depth of two feet[1].

In the same year, Swindon New Town arranged to maintain the towpaths within the town to enable them to be used as public highways[1]. The Wilts and Berks was practically disused by 1895 and an extra blow fell when the GWR obtained their water from Kemble and their yearly payment of £300 ceased abruptly[1]. This happened on completion of the laying of a water main from the Kemble boreholes to the Swindon works in 1903[98].

In 1898, the Syndicate, at last convinced that the canal could not be made to pay, applied for a warrant of abandonment[1]. This was opposed by Swindon New Town because they claimed water rights, because the towpaths had become a right of way and because they had built the wharf near Milton Road Bridge[1]. Wiltshire County Council, various land-owners, and neighbouring waterways also opposed closure[1]. Later in 1897 Swindon New Town UDC offered to buy the part of the canal in its area, but although the Syndicate was practically bankrupt, they would accept nothing less than £20,000[1]. This the UDC was not prepared to pay. The abandonment policy finally failed on a technicality[1].

By 1898 there was no traffic on the eastern end and only 8,168 tons west of Swindon[1]. In the same year a footbridge connecting Marlborough Street and Joseph Street (GR 143843), roughly midway between Kingshill Road Bridge and Cambria Bridge, was erected by the Corporation. Undated plans of this bridge are held in the County Records Office[51] and these show that no attempt was made to narrow the canal to shorten the span required, as had been the case with the road bridges. Instead the bridge had a clear span of 47 ft between brick abutments. The bridge itself was of steel girder construction with 4 ft high sheet steel panelled sides. These sides, instead of ending square, curved elegantly through a quadrant to meet the top of the abutments vertically. The footwalk was 6 ft wide and was approached by 16 brick steps up from the north bank and 13 steps from the south bank. The bridge deck is shown as being surfaced with 2 in blue bricks above 4 in of concrete. Vertical steel rails with bannisters (with scroll ends) ran the full length of the steps on each side. The total length of the bridge, including the steps, was 70 ft 6 ins. An elderly lady who had lived in Albion Street since her birth there in 1896, told me that she used to cross the bridge on her way to school (ie, during the period 1901-1910). "The bridge had wooden steps, twelve on each side. The decking was also wooden, but the side rails were sheet iron or steel".

This reminiscence is somewhat at variance with the bridge plans described above, particularly in regard to the use of wood instead of brick for the steps and decking. Whether this is an aberration of the memory or whether the local board made economies after the original plans were drawn up and switched to wood instead of brick must remain a matter for conjecture.

According to one source[57], before the footbridge was built, people used to cross the canal at this point by putting planks across it. They must have been large planks to span 37 to 40 ft and crossing must have been somewhat hazardous as planks of this length would have dipped considerably under a person's weight at the middle of the crossing.

In 1900 the 2nd Edition of the 1/2500 (25.344 inches to the mile) Ordnance Survey maps appeared, with revisions to 1898/1899. Several of these are held by Swindon Reference Library, but not a complete coverage, such as that held at the Ordnance Survey headquarters at Southampton. These maps show many of the developments already referred to, namely the development of the Rollestonc Estate, the replacement of Black Bridge by Milton Road Bridge (called Commercial Road Bridge on the map) (Sheet XV8) and the new Marlborough Street/Joseph Street footbridge (Sheet XV7). As stated earlier, no steps or slopes down to canal level at Milton Road Bridge are shown. Steps are shown on the south eastern side of the entrance to the Central Club (ie, the side furthest away from the canal). The entrance to the Club is at road level, so these steps provided access to the side of the building at canal bank level (and were still there in 1982). The west side of Albion Street is shown completely built up (following the vacation of Webb's timber yard) on Sheet XV7, but Joseph Street, although marked out, is not yet built up. This sheet also shows the widened Cambria Bridge, and an area just north of the approach from Westcott Place is designated Cambria Recreation Ground. Steps lead down to it from the bridge approach and both the Recreation Ground and the steps are still there today. The 1900 map shows the eastern side of Cambria Bridge Road to have been developed since the 1886 Edition was published, and also Curtis Street, which parallels the canal from its junction with Cambria Bridge Road to Milton Road. A local source[57] suggests that the brick terraces of Curtis Street were built in the period 1886-1889.

Sheet XV4 includes the Golden Lion Bridge and still shows only one footbridge on the north east side, as on the 1886 edition. Since two footbridges were shown on a photograph taken in 1904 (see below), the second footbridge, on the south west side of the lifting span, must have been erected very soon after the map was compiled, ie, between the map revision date of 1898/1899 and 1904. Also shown is the wharf near to Milton Road Bridge, just north of the Central Club alongside Wharf Road. It is marked "Wharf UDC". A painting of Cambria Bridge viewed from the south west at about this date (1895-1900) was reproduced in the Swindon Evening Advertiser in September 1978[58] and was titled "Marlborough Street to Cambria Bridge". The view is directly along the canal line and shows the back gardens of Albion Street running down to the canal on the south eastern bank, and the steeply sloping embankment carrying the towpath above the lower ground to the north west. A photograph of the modern scene was also shown for comparison.

A photograph of the junction with the North Wilts Canal, taken in 1900, is held in Swindon Reference Library. The view, which is towards the east in the direction of Queenstown and Whale Bridges, shows the canal to be full of weeds.

In 1904 the Golden Lion Bridge (and Fleet Street Bridge on the North Wilts) was strengthened prior to the opening of the Swindon Tramway system in September of that year[6].

A photograph of the Golden Lion Bridge taken in 1904 was reproduced in the Wiltshire Star in September 1978[58]. It is an excellent close up looking from where the British Home Stores building stands today, and shows the raised footbridges with ornate wrought iron trellis work side rails, the lifting beams and pillars and the wrought iron lattice work fencing of the main span at street level. The capstan which operated the lifting gear is also visible at the Regent Street end of the span. Several children in their Sunday best are standing on the steps of the footbridges at the Bridge Street end. The canal is free of weeds and the abutments can be clearly seen. Lloyds Bank is visible in the background on the Regent Street side of the bridge. Another photograph taken in 1905 looking across the bridge towards Bridge Street is in the slide collection of Swindon Museum[21], and shows a tram approaching. The footbridges are still in position. This view has been published as a postcard by the

Museum (Fig. 10) but the field of view excludes the footbridges. Yet another photograph of the same vintage is held by Swindon Reference Library.

Fig. 10: Tram approaching Golden Lion Bridge, 1905 (Swindon Museum Collection)

Another early photograph of the bridge, which also shows the footbridges, appeared in Swindon "Evening Advertiser" in 1964[20] and shows the view looking directly across the bridge up Regent Street. A clear view of the footbridges shows seven steps up each side, and a width of some 6 - 8 ft. The accompanying description states that the bridge was "winched up horizontally by two men".

In 1906, part of Stanley aqueduct (the largest on the canal) which carried the canal over the River Marden near Calne, collapsed causing a loss of water from the canal and the cessation of all traffic[1]. The aqueduct was never repaired and the canal was dead. With the need to raise it having disappeared, the Golden Lion Bridge became to all intents and purposes a fixed bridge, and the raised footbridges were removed in 1906, being replaced by level footpaths[6].

Plans held in the County Record Office[51], dated 29th April 1907, may be related to this conversion. The plans are headed "Borough of Swindon. Regent Street Bridge Proposed Improvement", and show the proposed addition of a cantilevered footpath on each side, 5 ft 6 in in width, attached to the main span by steel girders. The position of one of the former footbridges is shown by dotted lines. The bridge span itself is shown to be decked with pitch pine.

Swindon Corporation spent £1,500 in 1908 dredging the 3¾ miles inside the borough but it was soon choked again with weed, mud and rubbish[1]. The Royal Commission on canals and inland navigations presented its report in December 1909. It commented on the Wilts and Berks: "It was largely used within living memory for the transport of coal, corn, building and road making materials. Now it is absolutely unused and its banks are dilapidated. The company which owns it makes a small revenue, insufficient to meet expenses, by the sale of water. The stagnant condition of this canal makes it offensive to the people of Abingdon and Swindon and a desire has been expressed in these towns to close it altogether and fill in the bed. This closing is, however, opposed by the landowners for certain reasons, including the fact that their tenants obtain water from it for their cattle."[1]

Proposals to convert the old arch bridges at Drove Road and Kingshill Road to wider steel bridges on the lines of Cambria, Queenstown and Whale bridges were drawn up by the Borough Council in 1912, the plans now being held in the County Record Office[51]. Only the plan of Drove Road Bridge is dated - at June 1912, but it is fairly certain that the Kingshill Road Bridge plan is of similar vintage. However, these bridges were still owned by the Canal Company and such alterations were necessarily subject to their agreement. In the event, these proposals were overtaken by moves to close the canal.

Action to close the canal in Swindon was started in 1912 by the promotion of a Bill in Parliament by Swindon Corporation. W J Ainsworth, the United Commercial Syndicate canal manager, was called to give evidence before the Parliamentary Committee[1]. He stated that the canal had 165 bridges of various types, and that the paid up capital of the owners was £17,000. The canal was dry in places, especially on the North Wilts branch; bridges were dangerous, often blocking the canal. Numerous locks were in ruinous and unworkable condition and towing paths were overgrown. He submitted a series of photographs to substantiate his evidence[1].

Several photographs of 1910-1912 vintage are held in Swindon Reference Library, including some stamped Swindon Corporation on the back, and it is probable that these were the photographs submitted by Ainsworth to the Parliamentary Committee[16]. Certainly, all of them show the canal in a dilapidated condition and three are reproduced in Dalby's book[1], including views of Swindon Wharf and of John Street Bridge on the North Wilts. One held by the Reference Library (dated 1910) of Kingshill Road Bridge shows the stone arch bridge as depicted on the earlier paintings held in Swindon Museum. Another shows the Marlborough Street/Joseph Street footbridge viewed from the south western side.

A photograph taken from the junction with the North Wilts Canal looking along the main canal towards the Golden Lion Bridge is shown in Fig. 11. Notice the absence of the raised footbridges by the bridge, following their removal in 1906. The building on the extreme left is College Street School built in 1873.

The Swindon Corporation Closure Bill finally became law on 31st July 1914, and authorised the transfer to the Mayor, Aldermen and Burgesses of the Borough of Swindon the site of a portion of the Wilts and Berks canal and Coate reservoir (which was originally built to supply water to the canal via a feeder joining the canal at a point just west of the present Greenbridge Industrial Estate), and the abandonment of the remainder of such canal and the sale of disposal of the site thereof[1].

Fig. 11: Junction with the North Wilts Canal and Golden Lion Bridge c 1911

The Corporation acquired all the canal property in Swindon, including Coate, for £10,000. Outside the Borough owners of land abutting the canal had it vested in them free of charge. All bridges and the land beside and beneath these were vested in the Authority owning the roads. Similarly, the GWR was vested with the sites of railway bridges and canal property beneath them[1].

So ended the active life of the Wilts and Berks and North Wilts canals. Although the canals could not be called financially successful, they played their part in the development and prosperity of Wiltshire and Berkshire.

Even if the Borough Council had intended to proceed with the 1912 proposals to improve Kingshill Road (and Drove Road) bridges, the commencement of the Great War within a month of their acquisition prevented the proposals getting beyond the drawing board.

## 1914 to the Present

Not much was done to the old canal until after the Great War finished in 1918. In that year, as part of the improvements made to the Swindon tramway system, the Golden Lion Bridge was replaced by a solid embankment[6]. Two transparencies taken from photographs illustrating the work in progress are held by Swindon Museum[21]. The original photographs were taken in opposite directions looking up and down Regent Street and show soldiers in uniform working amongst the labourers (the Great War was drawing to an end at this time). The photograph looking north towards Bridge Street is the most informative and shows the eastern pillars of the lifting mechanism with a steel girder spanning the tops of the pillars. The only other evidence of the original bridge is the side railings just alongside the lifting pillars, at street level. The Golden Lion effigy is to be seen on top of the pub of that name, and a poster on a nearby hoarding advertises an event to be held on Monday, 1st July 1918.

There was considerable discussion in the town in the early twenties about what should be done with the canal. This is referred to in Norman G Liddiard's commemorative essay "The Borough of Swindon 1900-1974"[19] "One view was that it should be turned into a decorative feature of the town's landscape. The opposing view held that it should be filled in, and it was this view that carried the day. As a consequence the centre of the town was to sport little more than a rubbish tip for the next forty years or more."

An artist's impression of what might have been, had the proposal to convert the canal into a decorative feature been successful, is illustrated in a recent publication by the Swindon Society[97]. It shows a similar view to Fig. 11. There are tree lined promenades on both sides of the canal and in the centre of the canal junction is an artificial island with a canopied shelter or band stand on it. This is approached by bridges from both banks of the main canal. the title of the sketch is "Regent Street Canal and Promenade Swindon".

Several plans in a numbered sequence, of 1920 vintage, are held by the County Record Office[51] and indicate the council's intentions for the various canal bridges following the decision to fill in the canal. Only two of these plans are dated, both in February 1920, but since they are clearly a numbered set, they must all have been prepared at about the same time.

Taking the bridges on this section in sequence, the plans show the intention to convert Kingshill Road Bridge and Marlborough Street footbridge to embankments, whilst the only change to Cambria Bridge was to be resurfacing. Milton Road Bridge was not scheduled for alteration, and the Golden Lion Bridge had already been converted to an embankment in 1918. There was also a rather surprising proposal to built an embankment across the canal from Read Street, just NE of Marlborough Street. Whereas the latter connects to Joseph Street, there is nothing but the back gardens of Albion Street across the canal from Read Street, and it is difficult to see a need to connect the two, particularly with the Marlborough Street/Joseph Street crossing being so close at hand. However later OS maps show that the Read Street proposal was not implemented.

The plans all show the canal to be unfilled at this time (February 1920), but filling in of the canal must have started very soon after this, since the 1923 3rd Edition of the 1/2500 Ordnance Survey maps (revised 1922) shows the canal to be filled in from just south of Kingshill Road Bridge all the way to the junction with the North Wilts Branch, and beyond it as far as Queenstown Bridge. The towpath on the west bank of the filled canal is still indicated by dotted lines. Judging by photographs of other filled in sections of the canal, and the present day appearance, the infilling was most probably a mixture of earth, rubble and rubbish, roughly levelled to provide an area of waste ground alongside the towpath, which was metalled or at least better surfaced than the infilling since the towpaths first had to carry the traffic of the barge horses, and then later the pedestrians of Swindon.

The filling in of the canal obviated the need for an embankment to replace the Marlborough Street/Joseph Street footbridge, simple removal of the bridge and construction of a linking stretch of roadway between the two streets being all that was necessary. However, Kingshill Road Bridge had embanked approaches, and the bridge itself was on a skew relative to the approach roads, and the Council levelled the approaches, and widened and straightened Kingshill Road to remove the skew. Both of these alterations are shown on Sheet XV7 of the 1923 3rd Edition 1/2500 map. As stated earlier, Cambria Bridge and Milton Road Bridge were unaltered but a footbridge is shown across the abutments of the Okus/Rushey Platt bridge at GR138838. One source[61] has suggested that this footbridge was built in the 1914-18 war.

Sheet XV8 includes Milton Road Bridge and still gives no indication of steps or slopes down to canal level. However a line parallel to the canal side of the Central Club entrance may indicate the presence of steps down to the canal infill on this side of the entrance to match those already present on the other side of the entrance (and shown on the 1900 map). Up to the time of the demolition of the Central Club (August 1982) there were what appeared to be the remains of steps in this position, with a wrought iron entrance gate between the end of the bridge balustrade and the Club entrance. Map measurements indicate that the width of these steps (if this is what the line on the map represents) was about 6 ft.

Sheet XV4 shows the embankment which replaced the Golden Lion Bridge in 1918. At some date after the filling in of the canal the milestone "Semington 26 miles", which stood on the south eastern bank of the canal roughly mid-way between Milton Road and Regent Street, was re-erected at the rear of Lloyds Bank in Regent Street. A photograph of this milestone appears in Dalby's book[1].

A local source[82] states that there were steps down to the canal towpath from both sides of Milton Road Bridge at the Milton Road (NW) end between the wars, and that those on the south western side of the bridge were removed well before the 1939-1945 war, whereas those on the other side remained until just before the war, or until the early part of the war. No steps are shown on the 1942 1/2500 OS map, so this may indicate that both sets of steps had been removed by 1942.

Little changed on this section of the canal until the early 1960s when redevelopment of Swindon's shopping centre started. The filled in section at the junction with the North Wilts branch was in use as a car park as early as 1937/38, and air raid shelters were erected here during the 1939-45 war[10]. During the war the watered section of the canal south of Kingshill was dredged out to provide a reservoir for the Auxiliary Fire Service[29].

The 1942 revision of the 1/2500 Ordnance Survey maps sheets XV7 and XV8 showed remarkably little change from the 1923 3rd Edition. Both sheets were revised in 1942, and the only change visible is the renaming of the wharf adjacent to Milton Road Bridge as "Corporation Depot". (On earlier maps it was marked simply "UDC".) The footbridge at Rushey Platt is still shown. This footbridge appears to have been removed before 1946, in spite of it being shown on the 1951 (sheet 4/18) and 1959 (sheet 50/18) editions of the 2.5 inches to the mile OS maps. Direct evidence for this removal is provided by the 1946 RAF Aerial Survey photographs[84] which show no bridges between Kingshill Road and the Midland and South Western Junction railway bridge at GR137835. Not even the abutments of the old bridge remain.

In 1945, this section of the canal was cleaned out again and the towpath repaired to improve local amenity[4]. This clearance is evident on the aerial photograph, where the portion of the canal north of the railway bridge is much clearer of weeds than that to the south. The watered section ends about 20 yards short of Kingshill Road.

A further aerial survey was carried out in March 1948, at a lower level, and shows more detail than the 1946 survey. Three prints show the watered section south of Kingshill Road[85] and indicate some further infilling of the canal adjacent to this road, the infill now stretching for about 100 yds along the canal line towards the south west.

No other changes from 1946 are apparent, apart from the appearance of a structure across the canal some 260 yds from Kingshill Road. It is not possible to discern whether the structure is a bridge or a temporary dam. If the former it would have provided a short cut to the south western end of Hill's yard. If the latter, it could have been a prelude to further infilling, since the position corresponds closely with the end of the watered section today.

Whilst the old abutments and later footbridge at the Okus bridge site (GR138838) have gone, there is an indication of something, possibly rubble, in the water at this point. The line of the footpath leading up the hill from the southern end of the bridge site can be seen.

The 1948 aerial survey photographs also throw a little more light on the puzzle of Milton Road Bridge steps. Three prints show the bridge[86]. The lighting is from the south west, almost directly along the line of the canal, giving bright sunlight on the south western side of the bridge and deep shadow on the north eastern side. On the south western side there are no steps at the south western corner of the bridge (where there is thought to have been a slope); the area inside the side wall being partially grassed. At the north western corner, where there were steps, the area inside the side wall appears white and totally devoid of grass, as is the area at the lower end of the steps. The appearance is consistent with recent renovation or alteration, but the lighting is such that individual steps cannot be distinguished, and so the question of whether the steps were still there, or had recently been removed, cannot be answered. However the shadows of the bridge balustrade on this side of the bridge indicate that access to the slope and steps at the ends of the balustrade had not yet been blocked off, which would lend support to the view that they were still in use in 1948.

Although the steps on the opposite side of the bridge, at the Milton Road end, are in shadow, the side wall can just be discerned, and access to Milton Road has not been blocked off, (a bill hoarding was later erected here after the steps had been removed), which probably indicates that the steps were still in use.

By 1950, the Golden Lion effigy had been removed from the roof of the pub and re-erected on a plinth in the little walled garden adjacent to the pub's canal frontage. An article in the Swindon Evening Advertiser in 1977[62] states that the effigy was put on the roof of the pub in 1870, and was transferred to ground level when it became unsafe. This must have been after 1918, since the effigy was still on the roof in the photograph showing the demolition of the bridge in 1918, described earlier. The 1948 aerial survey photographs[87] show that the Golden Lion had been removed from the roof of the pub by this date and on one of the prints (5138) it is just possible to discern an object, which may be the effigy, at the NW corner of the bridge site, in the position where later photographs show it to have been re-erected.

A 1957 photograph (converted to a transparency) of the Golden Lion effigy at ground level is held in the Swindon Museum collection[21]. The view is from the present day site of British Home Stores, looking towards Milton Road. The canal line beyond Regent Street shows the tarmaced towpath on the right hand (NW) side, with the rest of the canal infill being grassed and tree-lined. The trees were probably remnants of the original hedgerows which lined the canal. Nearer to the camera, the canal line on the north eastern side of the bridge site is tarmaced overall, and a "No-Exit" sign suggests that it was used as a car park.

The Golden Lion pub closed on the 15th March, 1956[99], in anticipation of the redevelopment which was to follow five years later.

The 1958 Edition of the 25 inches to the mile Ordnance Survey map shows little change from the 1942 situation and a 1957 photograph of Kingshill Road shows the former site of the Bridge as it is today. The 1957 1/1250 Plan SU 1484 NE (surveyed March 1956) shows an alteration to the "steps" on the canal side of the Central Club entrance, indicating that they have been roughly halved in width (to about 3 ft) at the bridge entrance and narrow to virtually nothing at ground level. This corresponded with the situation up to the time of the demolition of the Central Club (August 1982), so it can be taken that these steps (if they were steps) were demolished between 1942 and 1956. This larger scale map clearly shows the side rails corresponding to the former site of the steps and slope on the south western side of the bridge, but the indication of the rails at the north eastern corner of the bridge cannot be distinguished from other map markings, although these rails are known to have been there right up to the reconstruction of the steps in 1977. A 1960 photograph of the site of the junction with the North Wilts canal shows the car park which had been there since the thirties. Both this photograph and the 1957 photograph of Kingshill Road are held by Swindon Reference Library.

Between 1961 and 1964 extensive redevelopment took place along the line of the canal in the immediate vicinity of the former site of the Golden Lion Bridge, both to the south and north of Regent Street. This became "The Parade", a shopping precinct which was the first stage in the architectural surgery aimed at producing a new shopping centre for Swindon.

A stone tablet in the centre of the Parade at the rear of British Home Stores states that the work commenced on the redevelopment on 14th April 1961. The article already referred to on page 26, describing the old "Golden Lion Bridge" which appeared in the Swindon Evening Advertiser on 10th August, 1964, was printed on the eve of the opening of extensions to the British Home Stores in the Parade.

The construction of the Parade involved the demolition of many buildings on both banks of the canal for a distance of 150 yards on each side of Regent Street. The Golden Lion pub, which had watched over the canal for 100 years, fell victim to the advance of modern Swindon. The Lion itself was carefully brought into storage with the intention of re-erecting it as a reminder of the old pub after completion of redevelopment. It was covered by a tarpaulin, but unfortunately this proved disastrous; frost effectively destroyed the effigy which had withstood nearly a century of Wiltshire weather, and when the tarpaulin was removed, the Lion had crumbled and shattered beyond the possibilities of repair[29].

All the 1861 terraces on the north west bank (Waterloo Terrace, Belwood Place, Alma Terrace and Albion Terrace) were demolished as were most of the buildings on the west side of College Street on the south east bank of the canal. Amongst the latter was College Street School, and a tablet let into the wall of a passage leading from the Parade into College Street (adjacent to the Tesco store) commemorates the event. The school was built in 1873 and demolished in 1962, but the tablet was preserved thanks to the good auspices of Dr Bruce Mortimer, former Deputy Education Officer for Swindon[63].

Some aerial photographs of Swindon taken in 1961, soon after work started on the construction of the Parade, are held by Swindon Museum. These show that access to the steps at the north east corner of Milton Road Bridge has been blocked off by a bill hoarding; this probably indicates that the steps had been removed by this date. The bill hoarding was still there in 1975, as shown in Fig. 12. In contrast to the earlier aerial survey photographs of 1946 and 1948, which were taken from vertically overhead, the 1961 photographs were taken from a lower altitude at an oblique angle. This effectively hides the south western side of Milton Road Bridge from view, preventing any information being gained regarding the steps and slopes on this side of the bridge. In the distance the watered section of the canal beyond Kingshill Road appears clear and weed free.

Fig. 12: Central Club and Milton Road Bridge, April 1975

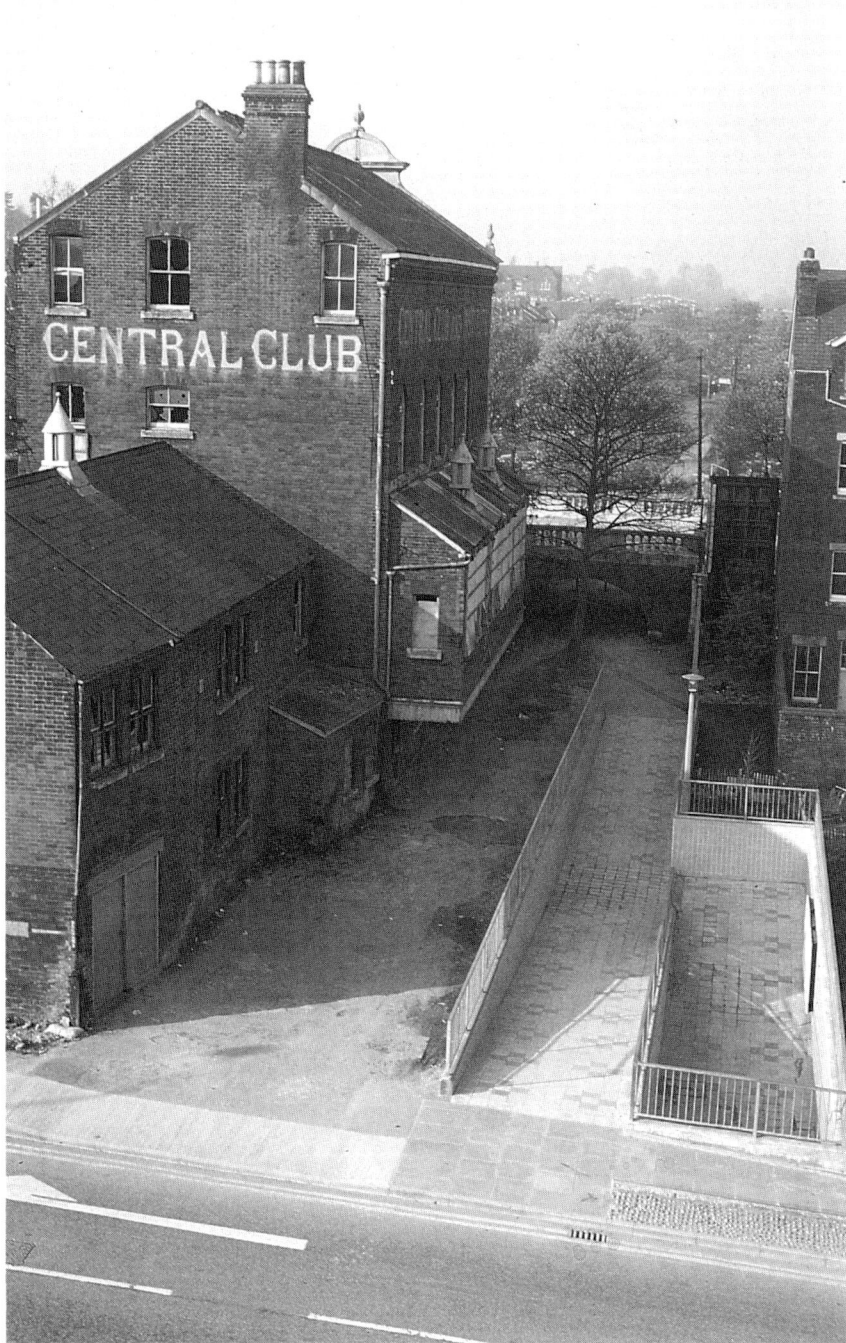

The 1966 edition of the 1/1250 Ordnance Survey series of plans (50:688 inches/mile), Plan SU 1584NW (revised 1965), shows the new Fleming Way dual carriageway, which follows the line of the North Wilts canal west of the junction, and the main canal east of the junction. Fleming Way was constructed during the period 1963-65 and forms the northern boundary of the Parade. The re- development in the vicinity of the Parade is also shown. The neighbouring sheet SU 1484 NE shows the former wharf site near to Milton Road Bridge to have been cleared of Corporation buildings and in use as a car park. The old Fire

Station building on the wharf site is still shown though. Some houses on the western side of Cromwell Street, adjacent to the wharf site (nos 14 to 18), have also been demolished.

In August 1967, Swindon Trades Council recommended that the Borough Council clean up the watered section of canal at Kingshill[64]. It is doubtful if this was done, because in 1970 the Swindon Isis Angling Club were granted a 15 year lease of the watered section of the canal south of Kingshill Road. They planned to dredge the canal and to re-stock it with fish[5]. The club hoped to get a 50% Government grant for the restoration; the estimated cost of dredging was £2,700.

About this time, probably during the summer of 1969, a further stretch of canal just south of the old Midland and South West Junction Railway bridge at Rushey Platt was filled in. This is indicated both by a slide held in the Swindon Museum collection[21] and by detail shown on the large scale OS maps of 1970 and 1976. The slide, which was taken in September 1969, shows the view from beneath the railway bridge looking towards the south. The end of the watered section and the beginning of the new infill can be seen. The infill is clearly very recent because it is bare of vegetation - a situation which would only persist for a few weeks at this time of the year. The 1970 1/2500 OS map (sheet SU 1383, surveyed 1955, further information added 1969) does not show the infilling, the canal being watered to the map edge from south of Kingshill. The 1976 1/1250 plan SU 1383 SE (revised 1975) shows the canal filled in from GR136831 to GR137833 (the northern end of infill shown on the slide).

By this time, the Cirencester/Swindon Old Town/Andover line which ran over the railway bridge had closed; the last passenger train having left Swindon Old Town for Andover on 10th September, 1961[65]. Some track was relaid in 1970 to accommodate roadstone transportation to the M4 construction; access from the main London/Bristol line being available via a spur at Rushey Platt junction just over a mile west of Swindon's main line station[54]. Recently (1978) the Swindon and Cricklade Railway Society has been formed with the intention of restoring the section of line between Moredon and Cricklade as a tourist attraction[66]. The section between Mannington and the former of the Old Town Station is now a pleasant pedestrian and cycle route, thanks to the efforts of Swindon Bike Group.

A 1968 photograph of the canal line adjacent to Swindon Market was reproduced in the Wiltshire Star[67]. The view looks towards the Central Club and Milton Road and the canal infill is tarmaced and in use as a carpark (the former Wharf site). The towpath is also tarmaced and is separated from the car park by a grassed verge lined with trees - probably those which lined the canal when it was watered. Photographs of this section of canal between Regent Street and Milton Road taken between July 1970 and March 1971 are included in the Swindon Museum collection[21] and show that the tree lined towpath ran all the way from Regent Street to Milton Road. Another car park was situated adjacent to the New Swindon Gas Works halfway between Regent Street and Milton Road. The canal here was higher than the lower ground to the north west (Catherine Street side) and there were steps down from the towpath level to another car park on the lower ground.

At some time prior to 1964, the steps down to canal level at the north west corner of Milton Road bridge were removed and their access from Milton Road fenced off. The exact date of their removal is uncertain, but it was almost certainly before 1956 since the 1/1250 OS Plan SU 1484 NE published in 1957 (surveyed March 1956) shows the steps to have been removed, but their retaining walls and side rails are still in position as they are today. This situation is illustrated in a slide held in Swindon Museum[21] taken in November 1964. On the south western side of the bridge, the space formerly occupied by the steps is an untidy scarp of earth, weeds and bushes.

Since October 1970 a large area immediately south of the former site of the Golden Lion Bridge has been redeveloped, to create a new complex of shops and offices called the Brunel Centre. The area affected extends to Havelock Street in the east and Commercial Road in the south. Cromwell Street, which ran parallel to and south east of the canal, has disappeared, as has the car park at its southern end, (the old Wharf site) in which the line of the canal was clearly visible. Slides taken during the demolition of Cromwell Street are held in the Swindon Museum collection[21], including one of the old Fire Station just before it was demolished.

Stage One of the Brunel Centre commenced on 17th December, 1970 and was completed on 29th March, 1973. This is recorded on the base of a statue of Brunel which has been erected in the "plaza" on the east side of the complex, near to the northern end of what remains of Havelock Street. Stage Two of the construction commenced in June, 1973 and involved the area nearer to Commercial Road. The shopping precinct running along the north western edge of Stage One has been named "Canal Walk".

During the summer of 1975, Youth Enterprise Swindon, a group of local volunteers, carried out a sponsored clean-up of the watered section of the canal at the foot of Kingshill[30].

Stage Two of the Brunel Centre, dominated by the massive 320 ft Murray-John tower, was completed in 1976. A plaque on the stairs leading up to the new Market from the central concourse below the Murray-John tower states that the final stage of the Brunel Centre was formally opened on the 19th November, 1976. The Murray-John tower is directly on the line of the western bank of the canal and in about the same position as the old Queen Street Gas Works, which was served by the wharf on the opposite bank. The Gas Works was demolished in August, 1973. These changes are shown on the 1976 OS 1/1250 Plan SU 1484 NE (revised September, 1975). In addition to the demolitions east of the canal line in the Cromwell Street area already referred to, extensive demolition west of the line also took place, with all the brick terraces in the area bounded by Villett Street (NW), Catherine Street (NE), the canal line (SE) and Farnsby Street (SW) being demolished in addition to the Queen Street Gas Works mentioned previously.

An access bridge linking the vehicle unloading area on the roof of the Brunel Centre (Stage One) with the Murray-John Tower complex was constructed during the Stage Two development.

The pedestrian way Canal Walk was planted with flower beds and trees in November 1975. The old canal milestone, formerly at the back of the Regent Street Branch of Lloyds Bank (now demolished) was re-erected at the western end of the Parade frontage of the then Peter Richards shop in February 1976 and is shown in Fig. 13. This corresponds to the north western bank of the canal, on which the towpath ran, and in this respect the milestone is incorrectly located. According to Dalby[46] all milestones were on the opposite bank to the towpath for easy sighting, so the original position at the back of Lloyds Bank, which corresponded to the south eastern bank, the opposite of the towpath, was a more correct location than the present one. As stated earlier, the original location was some distance further south, probably in the vicinity of Macdonalds frontage to Canal Walk.

Fig. 13: Canal Milestone, Canal Walk, June 1991

In the face of considerable protests from conservationists, Thamesdown Council decided in 1976 to close the Old Market and to convert it to a carpark. The Market was eventually closed in 1977 and the traders transferred to new premises in the Murray-John tower complex. Demolition started soon afterwards and the conversion to the present day car park had been completed by early 1978.

Perhaps stimulated by such municipal vandalism, the Wilts and Berks Canal Amenity Group was formed in October 1977 with the objective of preserving the remaining sections of the canal from further deterioration. The Group has been engaged on the restoration of the Kingshill section and also the sections just south of Shrivenham, and near to Wootton Bassett, amongst other projects.

Also in the autumn of 1977, the steps down to canal level at the north west corner of Milton Road Bridge were rebuilt to provide access to the pedestrian subway below Farnsby Street and the Brunel Centre multi-storey car park.

On a happier note, to celebrate the Queen's Silver Jubilee in 1977, Thamesdown Council decided to create a new "Golden Lion" to stand in Canal Walk right next to where the old one used to be until 1961. The new Lion was modelled by the late Carlton Attwood, the Swindon sculptor, and constructed from concrete reinforced by glass fibre by Messrs Gordon Allen and Edwin Horne[68]. The new Golden Lion was installed with appropriate ceremony on 24th February, 1978. In the Lion's stomach is a memories box, holding amongst other things, a copy of the Evening Advertiser, coins, photographs of the town's murals, a shopping list with current prices and various messages[68]. The Lion is shown in Fig. 14.

By 1978 the old steel girders of the 1893 Cambria Bridge were showing their age and Thamesdown Council decided to replace the central span. Reconstruction commenced on the 8th May, 1978 and was completed during the next three months. The original abutments were retained, but the span itself was replaced by a reinforced concrete platform, edged with brick parapets surmounted by steel railings (Fig. 15). In this respect the new bridge reverts to an appearance closer to that of the original 1877 Hinton bridge than its predecessor. Because the abutments have not been altered, the steel corner guard showing the rope marks has happily been retained. In 1981/82 a very attractive mural depicting canal scenes was painted on the northern side of Cambria Bridge by Mr Ken White for Thamesdown Council. This mural stretches down the full length of the embankment from the bridge itself towards Westcott Place.

Milton Road Bridge was renovated in April 1981. The old Bath stone balustrades were removed and replaced with concrete block balustrades and the abutments were given an extra facing of new brick work. The renovated bridge is shown in Fig. 16. In August 1982, the Central Club building (shown on the right in Fig. 16) was demolished and replaced by the present day office block.

Fig. 14: Golden Lion, Canal Walk, June 1978

Fig. 15: Present Day Cambria Bridge (reconstructed 1978), June 1991

Fig. 16: Present Day Milton Road Bridge (renovated 1981)
November 1981

## PRESENT DAY EVIDENCE OF THE CANAL

A series of slides taken over the period 1971 and 1981 of the present day evidence of the canal is held by Swindon Museum and may be viewed by appointment (Bath Road Museum, telephone Swindon 526161).

The following paragraphs and their contents in Sections II and III are written without reference to these slides.

Starting just south of the elegant skew bridge that carried the now closed Swindon Old Town to Cirencester line at GR 137835 (the old Midland and South Western Junction Railway), a watered section some 650 yds long stretches to within 300 yds of Kingshill Road. Apart from a short length used as a reservoir on the Rodbourne industrial estate, and the section beyond the former Moredon Power Station site, this is the only watered section of the canal remaining in Swindon.

The railway bridge is shown in Fig. 7 with the start of the watered section in the foreground. Just before the start of the watered section, some 50 yds south of the railway bridge, the River Ray runs beneath the canal under a stone aqueduct. If one is prepared to clamber through the undergrowth adjoining the towpath, one can still find the old aqueduct, much as it was when the canal was built. It is very solidly built, with two small arches through which the river flows. Apparently a popular teaser in the days when the canal was active was to ask how to get from New Town to Old Town without crossing the canal[45]. The answer was to use the aqueduct to go beneath the canal!

This section of the canal was the notorious Rushey Platt section which gave so much trouble to the builders of the canal in 1804[1]. It was described as "an area of quagmires which are considered to be of great depth and consequently shunned as places of danger". A noted geologist of the time, Dr William Smith, was consulted on how the canal could be carried through the moving bog "unhealthy and plagued"[1]. The crossing involved serious engineering difficulties and Smith was a frequent visitor to Swindon[10]. It is hard to imagine all this today when one walks along the towpath towards modern Swindon.

The canal bends sharply eastwards about 100 yds beyond the railway bridge to a straight section leading up to Kingshill Road. Just beyond the start of the straight section and about a quarter of a mile from the railway bridge, there is a gap in the hedge around a steel stile on the western side of the towpath. This is the site of the former access bridge (and later footbridge) to Okus. The footpath westwards to South Leaze is still in use, and there are indications of a footpath going steeply up the far bank of the canal on the opposite side, but there is very little direct evidence of the former bridge. A few bricks are scattered around the far bank, and there was (in 1972) the base of a sturdy 9 inch square wooden post sticking up from the bank on the towpath side. Whether the latter represented part of the footbridge dismantled in the 1940s is a matter for speculation. The degree of polishing that has occurred on the steel rails of the stile indicates prolonged and continuous use right up to the present time.

There is a slight hump in Kingshill Road where the canal line meets it (most noticeable if viewed from the vicinity of the junction with Westcott Place). This is all that remains of the much steeper hump formed by the old arch bridge that used to be over the canal.

The line of the canal continues towards the centre of Swindon beyond Kingshill Road as a clearly defined open space, with the central portion grassed, between the backs of Westcott Place and Albion Street. The footpath on the Westcott Place side is the former towpath and leads all the way to the Brunel Centre, and the hedge which adjoins it probably dates from the days when the canal was in use.

Over the period 1976-78, extensive demolition took place on the western side of Westcott Place, including virtually the whole of Westcott Street, and a long stretch of terraced houses south west towards Turner Street. Some 30 yds after leaving Kingshill Road, the footpath broadens into a back road used by the car owners of Westcott Place, and a similar back road has been created on the other bank of the canal at the rear of Albion Street. The filled canal bed is the grassed area in the centre, and was filled in by the early 1920s. About midway along the Westcott Place side is a back entrance to "The Falcon", a pub which undoubtedly served the bargees in its time.

Further on one comes to the road linking Westcott Place and Albion Street; this is called Marlborough Street at the Westcott Place end, and Joseph Street at the Albion Street end. This dual naming for an apparently continuous street is a reminder that it was once divided by the canal, and crossed by a footbridge. Nothing now remains to indicate the presence of this bridge (demolished in the early 1920s), the road crossing of the canal line being completely flat with continuous pavements on both sides. Only the gap in the houses and the peculiar dual naming provide clues to the past.

Moving further along the line, the canal bends east north east towards Cambria Bridge, some 250 yds away. Cambria Bridge was reconstructed in 1978, but the earlier version of this bridge, built in 1893, is shown from the northern side in Fig. 9. On the towpath side of the bridge (Westcott Place side) the brick abutments were protected from wear by iron plates, and the one on the Swindon (northern) side of the bridge is still in position. Closer examination of the iron plate shows rope grooves - perhaps the most evocative of all the relics of the old canal in this part of Swindon. The two most pronounced grooves are 7 ½ and 10 bricks up from the bottom of the abutment.

As stated earlier, because of corrosion of the steelwork, the central n of Cambria Bridge was replaced in 1978 by a reinforced concrete platform, with brick parapets surmounted by steel railings. The completed bridge is shown in Fig. 15, which can be compared with Fig. 9, which shows the bridge prior to reconstruction. Fortunately, the original abutments were retained, and the iron rope guard referred to earlier is still in position.

Since the bridge was rebuilt, a very attractive mural depicting canal scenes has been painted on the north side of the bridge and its abutments, which extends down the face of the embankment towards Westcott Place. This was painted in 1981/82 by Mr Ken White for Thamesdown Council, and provides a pleasant background for the children's playground below the bridge embankment.

The view north eastwards from Cambria Bridge is shown in Fig. 17, the towpath/footpath continuing along the left of the filled canal. In the distance the new buildings of central

Swindon can be seen, dominated by the Murray-John tower, which was being built at the time the photograph was taken (November 1975). The late 19th century terraces of Tennyson Street on the left and Curtis Street on the right are closer to the camera. In the middle distance a modern lamp-post can be seen at the side of the footpath, and if one looks immediately behind it the gaunt structure of the old Central Club (built 1897), which used to stand next to Milton Road Bridge (until its recent demolition) marks the line of the canal.

Until recent years, there were two notices between Cambria Bridge and Milton Road Bridge prohibiting cycling and driving along "the Towing Path" as a reminder of the old canal. These have now been removed, since the path is now a permitted route for cyclists.

Moving on towards the centre of Swindon, one comes to the most grandiose of all the canal bridges remaining in Swindon - Milton Road Bridge (Fig. 8 taken in February 1972, prior to the most recent renovation). This elegant and graceful Victorian structure must have been a source of pride to the locals when it was built by the Corporation in 1890. Immediately behind the tree on the right hand side of Fig. 8, the derelict Central Club building can be seen. This has since been demolished (August 1982). Milton Road Bridge used to have steps or slopes leading to the canal on both sides of the bridge. These have since been removed and the entrances to them fenced off from Milton Road, but the hand rails remain, clearly visible in Fig. 8.

However, in 1977, the steps at the north-west corner of the bridge were rebuilt to provide access to the new subway leading beneath Farnsby Street and the Brunel Centre multi-storey car park to Canal Walk and the Brunel Centre shopping area.

When it was first built, Milton Road Bridge had handsome wrought iron gas lamps on each corner pillar of the stone balustrades. These consisted of slender columns which supported the lamp globes at the top. Three of these columns still remained until the bridge was renovated in April 1981. Renovation consisted of refacing both sides of the bridge with an extra skin of new bricks, and replacing the old Bath stone balustrades with new concrete block and brick balustrades. The renovated bridge is shown in Fig. 16, taken in November 1981.

Fig.17: View from Cambria Bridge looking towards the Centre of Swindon, November 1975

Fig. 12 shows the rear view of the Central Club (and Milton Road Bridge) taken from the roof of the Brunel Centre multi-storey car park. This photograph was taken in April 1975, some three years later than Fig. 8, and shows the new subway beneath Farnsby Street in the foreground. The grassed area behind Milton Road Bridge is the canal line leading to Cambria Bridge.

Note the bill hoarding on the right hand side of Milton Road Bridge blocking off access to the former site of the steps down to canal level. New steps were erected here in 1977.

With the commencement of the construction of the Brunel Centre in December 1970, the next six years were to bring wholesale alterations to the appearance of the canal line from Milton Road to Regent Street. Stage One of this building work was completed in June 1973, and did not greatly alter the appearance of the line as it stood after the creation of the shopping precinct known as the Parade in the early 1960s. Stage Two of the Brunel Centre, commenced later in June 1973, produced far greater alterations, dominated by the Murray-John Tower, and that section of the Parade lying on the Milton Road side of Regent Street has now been renamed Canal Walk.

A March 1972 view of the south western end of the Parade (as it then was) is shown in Fig. 18. The grassed area and the brick building (Lloyds Bank) on the right disappeared in Stage Two development. The intersection of the Parade with Regent Street marks the former site of the Golden Lion Bridge, whilst the Golden Lion pub itself would have been at the far end of the row of shops in the left foreground. At the time this photograph was taken, the canal milestone illustrated in Dalby's book[1] was to be seen in the wall of Lloyds Bank, bearing the words "Semington 26 miles". It has since been re-erected in Canal Walk and is shown in Fig. 13, adjacent to the Miss Selfridge shop.

Fig. 14 shows the new "Golden Lion" installed in Canal Walk in February 1978 to commemorate the Queen's Silver Jubilee in 1977. The view is from the former site of the Golden Lion Bridge, looking south west along Canal Walk (and along the canal line) towards Milton Road. The old "Golden Lion" effigy used to rest on a plinth in front of the Golden Lion pub which would have been just out of picture to the right, where the Miss Selfridge shop is now. The restored canal milestone can be seen above the middle of the Lion's back alongside the shop entrance.

The Parade beyond Regent Street to Fleming Way follows the line of the old canal. The former site of the junction with the North Wilts Canal is where the Parade meets Fleming Way. The latter follows the line of the main canal eastwards and the North Wilts branch westwards (towards Fleet Street), and a view of the junction site is shown in Fig. 19. This was taken in May 1972 and the actual site of the junction would have been in the centre of the Parade, just beyond the far end of the subway, where the cyclepark is, mid-way between Bon Marche and Fine Fare (as they were then). The northern bank of the canal would have been where the subway starts on the far side of Fleming Way. Beyond the shops of the Parade in the foreground, the canal line westwards towards Kingshill is marked first by the trees at the far end of the Parade, then by the old Central Club building, just below the horizon slightly right of centre, and directly in line with the Fleming Way lamp-posts. The foreground scene has changed little since 1972, the only changes being the renaming of Bon Marche as Debenhams, and the replacement of Fine Fare by Primark. Looking at this scene, it is difficult to imagine the rural surroundings and relative tranquility of the canal's early days. The scene is also very different from that in the final days of the canal - Fig. 11, p. 28.

Fig. 18: The Parade (now Canal Walk), March 1972

Fig 19: Site of Former Junction with
North Wilts Canal, May 1972

## SECTION II:
## WILTS AND BERKS CANAL FROM THE FORMER JUNCTION WITH THE NORTH WILTS BRANCH TO THE EASTERN OUTSKIRTS OF SWINDON (GRID REFERENCE 151849 TO 185861)

## HISTORY

### 1794-1841

The hand drawn 20 inches to the mile map of the Wilts and Berks Canal held by Swindon Reference Library, which is thought to be the 1794 survey map[9] shows seven bridges on this section. As stated earlier in Section I, the showing of these bridges indicated an intention to construct, since the canal was not constructed until 1804.

The seven bridges are Whale Bridge (GR 153849), Drove Road Bridge adjacent to Swindon Wharf (GR 159 849), a bridge at GR 162850 carrying a track leading from Marsh Farm to buildings and fields south of the canal, a minor bridge at GR 165853, Green Bridge (GR 172860), Nythe Road Bridge (GR 180860) and Stratton Wharf Bridge (GR 185861). There is a widened section of canal on the west side of Green Bridge.

Four of these bridges - Whale Bridge, Drove Road Bridge, Marsh Farm Bridge and Stratton Wharf Bridge - were stone arch bridges, whilst the remainder were probably wooden drawbridges, on the evidence of the Canal Company's Works Ledgers (see below).

Whale Bridge is referred to in the Wilts and Berks Works Ledger B of 1804 as the "arched bridge at Eastcott" and is noted as being in the process of embankment at that time. It carried a road from Old Town to Lower Eastcott Farm.

It appears to have been the usual practice for bridges carrying important roads over the canal to be of stone construction, at least in the vicinity of Swindon where good quality stone could be quarried on Kingshill. Morris, in his book "Swindon Fifty Years Ago"[30] states "About the beginning of the 19th century, when the whole of the space on the western brow of the hill towards Westlecott was excavated, quarrying was reckoned never to have been so busy". A principal cause of this activity was the building of the Wilts and Berks canal which used Swindon stone in the building of the bridges, the erection of the canal office house at Swindon Wharf, and the paving before buildings on neighbouring wharves[32].

Drove Road Bridge is also referred to in the Works Ledger of 1804[10]; it carried the turnpike road to Cricklade and was referred to as the "Turnpike road bridge by Swindon Wharf". It must, therefore, be concluded that both Whale Bridge and Drove Road Bridge were built in 1803/1804.

The origins of Marsh Farm bridge, which is the only one of the seven bridges still in existence today, are more uncertain. The reference to it in Works Ledger B of 1806[10] is confusing in the context of its present day appearance. It will be seen from Fig. 22, p. 66, that the bridge is a stone arch, and, on the evidence of contemporary paintings, is similar in this respect to both Whale Bridge and Drove Road Bridge. Works Ledger B of 1806, however, refers to "carpenter making draw bridges at road at Eastcott, Marsh Farm ..."[10], which would imply a wooden drawbridge as a precursor of the stone bridge. Dalby is of the opinion that the present day bridge was in fact built at the same time as Whale and Drove Road bridges in 1804[9], which would mean that the reference to a wooden drawbridge in Works Ledger B is in error.

In fact it has been suggested[52] that whilst the canal company may have wished to build a wooden bridge for reasons for economy, Marsh Farm happened to be on the estate of Ambrose Goddard, who was a Director of the Company and the most influential man in Swindon at the time. He may well have insisted on a stone bridge being built. Support for this conclusion is given by a further 1806 entry in Works Ledger B which refers to the cost of "Spandrills at the bridges at Hay Lane, Kings Bridge, Chas Bradford's Bridge, Swindon wharf and Mr Barret's bridge at Marsh Farm £9-10s-0d. Since "Spandrill" is an architectural term used in connection with arches, it can be assumed that all of these bridges were arch bridges. Barret was the tenant farmer at Marsh Farm, and Bradford was the tenant farmer at Lower Eastcott Farm, confirming that this reference was to Whale Bridge[52].

The 1818 Ordnance Survey two inches to the mile drawing no 166 shows all seven bridges, together with an extra one between Nythe Bridge and Stratton Wharf Bridge at GR 182860. Later maps show this bridge in open fields, with no tracks or paths leading to it, and no buildings in the immediate vicinity. It can therefore be concluded that it was of minor importance, and in all probability it was a wooden drawbridge. Support for this view is given by an entry in Works Ledger B of 1806[52] which states "Making drawbridges at Stratton road, two in the fields at Stratton. Building an arched bridge at the Roman road near Stratton". As the last bridge mentioned is without doubt Stratton Wharf Bridge, the other three bridges must be respectively Green Bridge, Nythe Bridge and the bridge at GR 182860.

With the exception of Marsh Farm Bridge, and the bridge at GR 182860, all of these bridges are shown on the 1828 first edition of the one inch Ordnance Survey map[12]. The map markings are too indistinct in the case of Marsh Farm Bridge and the GR 182860 bridge to determine whether or not they are shown, but since this map was prepared from the 1818 two inch drawing, which did show both bridges, it can be safely assumed that they were there. The only development shown on this section of the canal was in the vicinity of Swindon Wharf.

Stratton Wharf Bridge is shown on a painting in Swindon Museum (undated, but probably 1880/1890 vintage) as a stone arch bridge.

Also shown on the 1828 map is the canal feeder from Coate reservoir, which was built in 1822, some two miles south of the canal, south east of Old Town, to provide extra water for the canal, the existing water supply having been found inadequate to meet the extra demands of the North Wilts branch which was opened in 1819 (see Section III). The feeder joined the canal at GR 167855, just north of the River Cole (which parallels the canal here) which was crossed by an aqueduct.

The construction of the reservoir which is nowadays a well known local feature, followed an unsuccessful attempt to use an artesian well sunk just east of the junction with the North Wilts, on the north bank of the canal at GR 152849. This well was sunk on the advice of Dr

William Smith the geologist who advised on the problems of Rushey Platt[1] (See Section I). The well was driven down several hundreds of feet to the Kimmeridge clay level, but the water, instead of gushing over the well top and then flowing under gravity to the canal, stopped at a level some feet lower. In the hope that the supply would nevertheless be adequate, a steam pump was installed, but this rapidly emptied the well, which then took several hours to refill. The scheme was abandoned[8]. The building in which the steam pump was housed was a large square building called "Canal House"[31], and it must have been built between 1819 and 1822. The building appears in the background of an 1885 painting of Queenstown Bridge[2], and also in a 1957 photograph taken from a similar viewpoint in a recent publication on Swindon's Public Houses[99]. William Morris' reference to the building (Reference 31) as "Canal House" is somewhat different to the description given in Reference 99. The latter states:

> "This imposing stonebuilt canal-side building was probably erected around 1841 by Rowden's of Highworth. It must have opened as a Beerhouse as William Smith applied unsuccessfully for a spirit licence in 1847. The 1851 census shows the premises empty.

> They then become a private house known variously as "Elm Villa" or "The Spur". At one time it was occupied by Samuel Carlton the GWR Works Manager. From 1905 to 1919 it was owned by the Lamb Brewery of Frome, and known as the "Engineers Arms". It was acquired as a private house in 1919 by the Preater family. The premises were finally acquired by Swindon Borough Council in 1960 and subsequently demolished. The main Post Office now stands on the site."

The 1957 photograph is captioned "The Engineers Arms, Wellington Street, in 1957 looking east along the Canal site. Whale in distance."

Since William Smith is the common factor in both descriptions, one may speculate that the dating of construction (1841) in Reference 99 may be incorrect, and that, following the failure of the artesian well project, Dr Smith sought an alternative use for the building, as a beerhouse.

The Victoria County History of Wiltshire[2], describing this period of Swindon's history, states "Northwards the Cricklade road ran through enclosed ground in its present course, now called Drove Road. At the north end it crossed the Wilts and Berks Canal at Swindon Wharf, where was the house of the manager; 'a villa, surpassing the second and approaching the first class' as Cobbett described it in 1826. Beyond the canal the road towards Stratton St Margaret turned off."

Referring to what later became known as Whale Bridge, VCH[2] says "At the northern end of Cow Lane was a swing bridge over the canal, beyond which an unfenced track led along the edge of fields to Lower Eastcott Farm, on a site occupied in 1964 by the omnibus depot". The reference to a swing bridge must be in error since Works Ledger B of 1804 clearly refers to an arch bridge[10], as mentioned earlier.

## 1841-1914

In the 1840s (about 1842) a terrace of 12 houses called Cetus Buildings was built in a close called Little Medgbury (near where Medgbury Road is today) and also "The Whale" beerhouse[2], which gave Whale Bridge its name. ("Cetus" is Latin for Whale.) The building was financed by the canal company. The Whale opened as a beerhouse, possibly in 1842, and was let to one Jonas Head[59].

Whale Bridge is shown as a stone arch bridge in the 1849 paintings of "New Swindon" on display in Swindon Museum and the Railway Museum, but the Little Medgbury development is not shown. Swindon Wharf is shown, together with Drove Road Bridge and one building (presumably the Canal Manager's villa) adjacent to it. Beyond this, the paintings are rather indistinct, but they do show the widened portion of canal adjacent to Green Bridge (GR 172861). Drove Road Bridge is shown as an arch bridge, but the configuration of bridges further east, including Green Bridge, cannot be distinguished. At this time (1840s) Swindon wharf was known locally as "Dunsford's Wharf", this being the name of the Canal Manager at the time[52].

In 1851 New Swindon consisted of Westcott Place and Street, the railway estate, and the groups of houses adjoining the station, the Golden Lion and the Locomotive (Fleet Street), the Union Railway and the Whale public houses[2].

An 1850 watercolour of Drove Road Bridge was exhibited in the "Farewell Swindon Borough" exhibition in 1974[14] and showed a stone arch bridge. Another undated watercolour at this exhibition showed Whale Bridge to be a very similar stone arch bridge.

According to Smith[3], a wharf had been built adjacent to Whale Bridge by 1857. This was known as "New Wharf". VCH[2] states that "between 1871 and 1881 much building took place ... the Trowbridge Building Society built a road adjoining Cetus buildings in a narrow field near the canal called Medgbury. All these streets were considerably built up by 1875. It was probably the following year which saw the building of Princes Street between the end of Regent Place and the canal, this reducing Cow Lane to a back way. Many of the houses, said to be in Cow Lane at this time, must be the brick terraces which in 1964 still faced parts of Princes Street. Regent Place, demolished by 1964, may also have belonged to this period". The Cow Lane terraces have also been demolished since 1964.

Marsh Farm Bridge is depicted (in its present day configuration) on an undated painting held by the museum which depict canal scenes, all thought to date from about 1880/90. Other paintings in this group show Stratton Wharf Bridge (referred to earlier) and Queenstown Bridge (dated 1885). The view of Stratton Wharf Bridge is from the eastern side, and shows various buildings on the north bank.

Also in the group is a painted map of Swindon dated 1882, see Fig. 6, p. 17. Whale Bridge is shown but not Queenstown Bridge. Neither is Queenstown Bridge shown on the 1886 1st Edition of the 1/2500 Ordnance Survey map (Sheet XV4, surveyed 1883/4). Tapscott Mason[10] states that Queenstown Bridge was built in 1885, which would be consistent with map evidence just quoted. He states that the bridge was built by Swindon Corporation at a cost of £900, and may have been linked with the enlargement of Queenstown Infant School in the same year. Queenstown School was originally built in 1880, and remained as an island of old Swindon in an otherwise completely redeveloped area (GR 151849) until March 1993, when it was demolished.

The 1885 painting of Queenstown Bridge must therefore have been painted soon after the bridge was completed. It shows a flat span, sheet steel sided bridge on brick abutments, similar to the later 1893 version of Cambria bridge. The approach from Wellington Street on the north bank is embanked, whereas that from College Street on the south bank is at street level. The painting is reproduced in Vol IX of the Victoria County History of Wiltshire[2]. Just behind the bridge, the square shape of Canal House, which formerly housed the abortive artesian well and steam pump, can be seen. According to Reference 99 at this time (1885) the building was a private house. The bridge was only about 50 yards east of the junction with the North Wilts Canal. Later, the bridge became more commonly referred to as Wellington Street Bridge[69].

Swindon New Town Local Board plans of this period, held by the County Record Office[51], show that several alternative designs for Queenstown Bridge were considered prior to its erection. Besides the design eventually selected (undated), the plans include two foot-bridges - one in steel (dated May 1884) and the other in wood (undated) - and a road bridge of shorter span than the chosen bridge, dated 7 April 1881. The selected design had foot-paths on both sides of the roadway, but in the event only the one on the west side of the bridge was constructed. The chosen bridge had a clear span of 27 ft, with the canal being narrowed from an original width of 38 ft to 20 ft to provide a foundation for the northern abutment and re-routed towpath. A later plan dated December 1887 shows a scheme to construct a cantilevered extension to the east side of the bridge to carry a second footpath, but this was not proceeded with.

An excellent photograph of Queenstown Bridge taken from the eastern side (the 1885 painting was from the western side) was published in the Swindon Evening Advertiser in 1977[74]. It is undated, and titled "Wellington Street Bridge", and is stated to be a reproduction of a postcard. The complete absence of weeds in the canal, and the good state of repair of the canal banks and towpath indicates that the photograph must have been taken soon after the bridge was built. A substantial building in the foreground (later to become the Queenstown Working Mens Club[75]) has only a narrow garden separating it from the south bank of the canal, whilst the end of the building faces College Street.

People are walking along the towpath on the opposite (northern) bank. According to a later correspondent, the photograph must have been taken from a side walk at the back of Queenstown School[75].

The 1886 1st Edition of the 1/2500 Ordnance Survey maps show all but one of the other bridges previously referred to on this section of the canal - Whale, Drove Road, Marsh Farm, Green Bridge, Nythe and Stratton Wharf, together with the bridge between the last two at GR 182860. However, the bridge at GR 165853, between Marsh Farm Bridge and Green Bridge, has gone, the only indication of its former presence being a narrowing of the canal at the site. (Sheet XV4, surveyed 1883/84.) A building is shown on the south bank of the canal at this point.

The bridge at GR 182860, shown on Sheet XV1.1 (surveyed 1874/83), appears to have been only an access bridge, since no tracks or footpaths are shown leading to it, and the land on either side of the canal consists of fields. The towpath appears to be at the same level as the bridge (on the south bank) which would be consistent with a drawbridge, since the local terrain is very flat and would be unlikely to provide high enough banks to permit a fixed bridge to be used.

Sheet XV1.1 shows the section of canal from Green Bridge to Stratton Wharf (which is marked as such) and no buildings are evident except in the immediate vicinity of these two bridges. There is a corn mill, named as Stratton Mill, adjacent to the north west corner of Green Bridge. The widened section of canal to the west of the bridge is also shown.

Nythe Bridge has an embanked approach from the south and appears to go above the towpath, which may indicate conversion to a fixed bridge, possibly in a similar manner to Black Bridge which had already been converted to a fixed bridge by 1885 (see Section I). It is not possible at this scale to determine the detailed configuration of the bridge and hence its construction.

The buildings of Wharf Farm are shown adjacent to the stone arch Stratton Wharf Bridge. The distribution of these buildings and the adjacent trees corresponds with the painting held in Swindon Museum.

Sheet XV4 (surveyed 1883/84) shows several bridges on the North Wilts Canal (see Section III), the Golden Lion Bridge, Whale Bridge, Drove Road Bridge, and Marsh Farm Bridge. A corn mill is shown on the north bank of the canal opposite Swindon Wharf (GR 159849). Extensive development to the west of the Oriel Street/Whale Bridge/Princes Street axis is shown, but there is little east of this line, apart from the Medgbury Road development of 1871-81 referred to earlier. A portion of this map showing the central Swindon area is reproduced in Fig. 28, p. 82.

The area around Swindon Wharf is referred to as "Fairholm". Just to the west of the wharf a cocoa factory is shown, whilst further west a large area south east of Whale Bridge is occupied by a brick and tile works.

The corn mill on the north bank does not appear to have been worked for very long[2].

The larger scale 1886 1st Edition of the 1/500 Ordnance Survey town plans of Swindon (10.56 ft to the mile) clearly show the masonry (stone) arch configuration of Whale Bridge on Sheets XV4.22 and XV8.2 (surveyed 1885). Drove Road Bridge and bridges further east were outside the coverage of these plans, which were confined to the built-up areas of Swindon.

In 1893 Whale Bridge was rebuilt by Swindon Corporation at a cost of £1200[10]. The related plans, dated 8th August 1891, are held by the County Record Office[51]. The old stone arch bridge was virtually derelict at this time[10] and must have created considerable hindrance to traffic. It was replaced by a flat span sheet steel sided bridge similar to Cambria Bridge and the nearby Queenstown Bridge. The changed configuration of Whale Bridge is shown on the 1900 2nd Edition of the 1/2500 Ordnance Survey map (Sheet XV4, revised 1899) and on a photograph taken about 1900 which is held in Swindon Reference Library. The photograph shows the view east from the junction with the North Wilts Canal, and shows a weed-filled canal passing under Queenstown Bridge and the very similar Whale Bridge, with Skurray's Mill (see below) towering above the latter in the background.

Comparison of the 1900 2nd Edition (revised 1899) with the 1886 1st Edition of the 1/2500 maps, and a study of two 1961 photographs of Whale Bridge held by the Reference Library show that alterations were made not only to the bridge itself, but also the "Whale" public house and its environs. (Reference 99 states that it was partially taken down and re-erected in 1906.) A flight of steps from a canal side entrance down to the towpath was removed and replaced by a flight coming down from a gap between the front of the pub and the end of the bridge. The bricked up former site of the older steps can be seen on the photographs.

Superimposition of a tracing of the 1900 map over the 1886 map shows that the new steel span was 36 ft wide compared to about 15ft for the original bridge, with the western side of the span coincident on both the original and the replacement. This meant that all the extra width of the new span was accommodated on the eastern side, bringing it right in line with the western end of the "Whale" public house. The new steps down to the towpath conveniently fill the gap between the end of the bridge and the pub, and are shown on the 1900 map.

One of the 1961 photographs taken from east of the bridge appears to show a mixed stone and brick construction for the abutments, implying that the remains of the original stone bridge were supplemented by brick additions during reconstruction. My interpretation of this photograph is open to question, because much of the critical detail is in shadow, but it does appear that most of the brick additions are on the eastern side of the abutments, which would be expected as all the extra width was accommodated on this side of the bridge. However, readers better acquainted with the bridge will be able to settle this point more definitely. If no stone work was visible in the rebuilt bridge, then it must be concluded that little of the original bridge was retained. On the other hand, the reverse is true if appreciable stonework remained.

A transparency prepared from an old photograph of the "Whale" steps in their post 1900 configuration is included in the Swindon Museum collection[21], and shows 14 brick steps with iron side rails on the canal side.

Other new features compared to the 1886 map are the appearance of the urinals on Whale Bridge and near to the Golden Lion Bridge. The western end of Medgbury Road, opposite Cetus Buildings, which was shown marked out on the 1886 map, has now been built up, with a terrace of 13 houses. A letter published in the Wiltshire Star in 1978[70] states that the house fronts of Cetus Buildings (numbered 80 to 91, Medgbury Road - the pub was no. 92) faced away from the canal, but at the back there was a large yard which overlooked the canal and faced Skurray's Mill on the opposite bank. The towpath was on the north bank, adjacent to the yard, and the barge horses were tethered downstairs at the back of Cetus Buildings, whilst the bargees were accommodated upstairs. Flour was delivered to Skurray's Mill by the barges. Skurray's Mill was built in the same year that Whale Bridge was reconstructed - 1893 - adjacent to New Wharf[27]. A sketch of Cetus Buildings was also published in the Wiltshire Star in 1978[71].

A transparency copied from an 1890s photograph is held by Swindon Museum[21] and shows Skurray's Mill and its wharf.

This building had a relatively short life as a flour mill, becoming one of the first garages in Swindon by 1911, when Skurray's became Ford dealers[72].

A 1960 photograph of Wharf House, Drove Road, was displayed in the "Farewell Swindon Borough" exhibition in 1974[14], and the building certainly justified Cobbett's description[2], being an imposing stone built residence.

Other changes evident on the 1900 2nd Edition maps (compared to the 1886 1st Edition) are the removal of some trees adjoining the approaches to Stratton Wharf Bridge (Sheet XV1.1, revised 1898) which is now simply called Wharf Bridge, and the appearance of a boat house near to the bridge.

The disposition of trees in the undated painting held by Swindon Museum of Stratton Wharf Bridge (referred to earlier) confirms that it must have been painted before 1898.

Some fresh development is shown east of Oriel Street and Princes Street, particularly north of the canal in the Corporation Street/Manchester Road area, and the County Ground and Football Ground appear for the first time, just north of Drove Road Bridge. The farm to the south of Marsh Farm Bridge is now named "The Closes", whilst the farm to the north is named as "Swindon Marsh Farm". (Sheet XV4, revised 1899.)

Queenstown Infant School has been extended by the addition of an extra wing on the western end; an alteration which took place in 1885 to provide a separate girls' section[73].

Amongst the plans held in the Wiltshire County Record Office[51] is one dated April 1899 showing the level of the towing path between Rodbourne Road Bridge on the North Wilts and Drove Road Bridge on the main canal. This shows that the level of the towpath between John Street Bridge on the North Wilts and Wellington Street Bridge just east of the junction with the main canal was higher than elsewhere. On the main canal, the positions of Wellington Street Bridge, Whale Bridge, Medgbury Place and Drove Road are all marked.

By 1900 the farm track running north from Whale Bridge past Lower Eastcott Farm (just east of Oriel Street) had been made into Corporation Street, and during the next fourteen years extensive development of the area between Corporation Street and County Road to the east (the northward extension of Drove Road) took place[12] The beginnings of this development were evident on the 1900 2nd Edition 1/2500 Ordnance Survey map, as stated earlier. This area was completely filled, in the main with brick terraces, and encroachment on the southern bank of the canal involved the building of Newcastle, Portsmouth and Plymouth Streets and York Road. Another bridge over the canal was built in about 1907/08 connecting York Road on the south bank with Graham Street on the north bank, at GR 157849[10]. During the construction of this bridge, the canal was diverted temporarily to allow the foundations to be built[34]. After completion, this left a widened section of the canal on both sides of York Road Bridge, which has been wrongly construed by some to be a place for barges to queue, forgetting that canal traffic had ceased some one or two years earlier in 1906. The bridge was another flat span sheet steel sided bridge, similar to the nearby Whale Bridge, but more attractively designed with cloverleaf patterns cut out of the ten steel side panels, and broad slopes leading down to the towpath on the north bank of the canal. The span was carried on brick abutments (which still exist today), with the southern abutment jutting out halfway across the widened canal. At the ends of the steel sides were brick pillars surmounted by pyramidal coping stones. These details can be seen on various photographs of the bridge held in Swindon Reference Library. Two taken in the early 1900s from a point east of the bridge shows a derelict barge near the southern bank.

An undated Swindon Town Council plan of York Road bridge is held by the County Record Office[51]. Unfortunately, only a plan of the bridge is shown, with no elevations or sections. The title is "Graham Street Bridge", rather than York Road Bridge, presumably because at the time the bridge was built Graham Street was fully developed, whereas little development had taken place in York Road, and it had not yet been adopted by the Town Council. The slopes down to canal level on the north bank are labelled "Back Road". On the south bank, steps are shown leading down to the backs of York Road on both sides of the bridge approach, but the early photographs held by Swindon Reference Library show only a grassy slope (at least on the eastern side), so it must be assumed that either the plan was drawn some time after the bridge was built, or that the construction of the steps was delayed for some reason. The steps were necessary because York Road was on an embankment near to the canal, whereas the backs were at canal level. Another council plan, dated 12th July 1911 gives details of the sewering, levelling and paving of York Road; almost certainly associated with its adoption by the Council. The west side of York Road is shown to be built up, but the east side is only developed as far as Portsmouth Street, some 60 yds short of the canal. Steps down to the backs are shown, as indicated on the undated plan described in the previous paragraph. Both sets of steps have landings halfway down.

By previous standards, York Road/Graham Street Bridge was a large bridge. It had a span of 31 ft and a width of 42 ft.

The two photographs referred to earlier were taken from a viewpoint east of the bridge, on the towpath which ran along the north bank of the canal. From the state of the canal and the derelict barge, one photograph is clearly earlier than the other, and must have been taken soon after the bridge was built, since no houses are to be seen in York Road, whereas the later photograph does show houses on the western side only (Fig. 20). On both a hedgerow adjacent to the towpath hides the slopes of the "back road" which paralleled the towpath from view, but in the later photograph it is just possible to discern the brick facing of the slope on the western side of the bridge. Later sketches and photographs show that this wall was topped with steel railings. On the south bank, a small copse of trees adjoins the bridge approach.

The Reference Library photograph reproduced in Fig. 20 also appears in the Swindon Society publication "Bygone Swindon" published in 1984[97].

The caption is "York Road Bridge 1912" and the description reads "This view from the bridge shows the 'ice breaker' slowly rotting; this iron bottomed boat was used locally to break ice, often by inviting the local children to rock the boat to and fro by jumping from one side to the other".

As stated in Section I, plans dated June 1912 held by the County Record Office[51] show proposals to convert the stone arch Drove Road Bridge to a steel girder bridge similar to Cambria, Queenstown and Whale Bridges, but this never materialised because of the advent of the Great War.

Other photographs of about 1914 vintage held by the Reference Library show Drove Road Bridge, still in its original stone arch configuration, and the nearby Swindon Wharf, now derelict and weedfilled, with half-sunken barges nearby (Fig. 21). The photograph of Swindon Wharf is reproduced in Dalby's book[1]. As stated earlier, these photographs were probably taken in support of Swindon Corporation's Closure Bill in 1914.

Fig 20: York Road Bridge, c 1912

One of the derelict barges shown in the photograph of Swindon Wharf is thought by R W May[69] to have been the ice-breaking boat, but this view is at variance with that expressed by Ref 97 which states that the derelict barge in Fig. 20 is the icebreaker. Apparently skating on the frozen canal was a popular pastime at the turn of the century. Once there was a near tragedy at the junction with the North Wilts when the ice gave way and hundreds of people were immersed[69]. When the ice was sufficiently thick, carts used to cross the canal at the end of Rosebery Street (just west of Drove Road) to avoid the long way round over the bridge[69]. This information was provided by Mr R W May, who used to live in the end house of Rosebery Street near to the canal until 1925[69]. Sketches by Mr May of Whale Bridge (1912), York Road Bridge (1922) and Drove Road Bridge (1918) appeared in the Swindon Evening Advertiser in 1978[76].

Fig. 21: Swindon Wharf c 1914

The view of Whale Bridge is from the east and shows Skurray's Mill with a barge moored alongside (artistic licence?), the "Whale" public house, and the steps alongside down to the towpath. York Road Bridge is viewed from the west and shows the canal in a somewhat weedy state; the slope down to the towpath on the north bank (Graham Street end) and the steps down to the backs of the western side of York Road on the south bank are also shown. Both sides of York Road are shown fully built up (1922), but the copse just beyond the bridge approach (which was evident on the early pre-war photographs) is still shown. Mr May maintains that there were no steps down to the backs of the eastern side of York Road at this time, the copse being on an area of waste ground[69]. This disagrees with the Swindon Council plan of 1911 described earlier, but agrees with the early photographs thought to have been taken before 1911.

Mr May's sketch of Drove Road Bridge (1918) is from the west, and a cottage situated alongside Drove Road at the northern end of the bridge is alleged to be the Old Toll House[69]. According to Mr May, from this house to Rosebery Street was a large bank formed by mud, etc, dumped from the canal dredger. Swindon Wharf was by this time known as Gilling's Wharf, this being the name of the firm renting the Wharf at the time[69].

## 1914 to the Present

As mentioned in Section I, little changed during World War I. Immediately after the war in 1919, the Garrard Engineering company established themselves in a small factory on the south bank of the canal just west of York Bridge Road, in Newcastle Street[43]. In the early twenties, before 1922, the canal was filled in with a mixture of earth, rubble and rubbish from Kingshill Road in the west of Queenstown Bridge in the east. As mentioned in Section I, several of the council plans relating to this phase of the canal's history are held by the County Records Office at Trowbridge[51]. A numbered sequence of plans prepared in 1920 show that Wellington Street (Queenstown) Bridge and Drove Road Bridge were to be lowered and converted to embankments, whereas Whale Bridge was merely to be re-surfaced and a new footpath constructed. No similar plans for York Road Bridge are held at the Records Office, possibly because it was the most recent of the bridges on this section and needed no alteration.

Three separate plans of the Wellington Street Bridge conversion, one dated September 1920, are held. They show that the road level was lowered by 6 ft, but nevertheless the top of the embankment was still 8 ft above canal level, which meant the construction of a special retaining wall to give clearance to the frontage of the Queenstown Working Men's Club at canal level. The roadway itself occupied the full width of the old bridge (20 ft 2 in), and new 5 ft footpaths were constructed on either side. Two of the plans show the canal to be watered on both sides of the embankment, whilst the third, presumably of later date, shows the canal filled on the west side and for a short distance on the east side, before the watered section commences. This probably indicates that the bridge was not demolished until after the canal had been filled in, ie, about 1921/23. It is believed that steps down to canal level were built into the embankment on both banks of the canal; the ones on the south bank provided a short cut to the Garrards factory further east, and also to the Queenstown Working Men's Club[77].

Two plans of the Drove Road Bridge conversion, both undated, (but one of which is in the numbered sequence some of which are dated February 1920), show the road level to be lowered by 5 ft after conversion, and widened from the 19 ft of the original bridge to 32.5 ft, not including 8 ft wide footpaths on each side. Because the canal was still watered, a 2 ft diameter culvert runs through the centre of the embankment.

The conversion of Drove Road Bridge to an embankment, and the in-filling of the canal to just east of the junction with the North Wilts as far as Whale Bridge, are shown on the 3rd (1923) Edition of the Ordnance Survey 1/2500 maps (25.344 inches to the mile), with

Sheets XV1-1 and XV4, both revised in 1922, showing the section under discussion. The fact that Sheet XV4 shows Wellington Street Bridge still as a bridge and not as an embankment, suggests that the subsequent conversion to the embankment illustrated on the Council plans did not take place until late 1922 or early 1923. Steps down from York Road Bridge to the backs on both sides of York Road are shown; this casts doubt upon the statement by R W May that there were no such steps on the east side of York Road in 1922[69]. Another section of the canal is shown to be filled in between Green Bridge and the point of entry of the Coate feeder, but all the rest remains watered with all bridges intact. According to Mr R W May[69], a dam was built across the canal at the point of entry of the Coate feeder (GR 167855), at the end of the filled section west of Green Bridge, to store the water from Coate reservoir, in about 1919. The local boys used to use it as a swimming pool. Until recently (1986), there was a reservoir at this point serving a factory on the Greenbridge industrial estate*. The canal itself is marked "Wilts and Berks Canal (Disused)"; various other buildings adjacent to the canal - Stratton Wharf and Stratton Mill (near Green Bridge) - are also marked "Disused". The boat house near Stratton wharf has gone, and the small access bridge just east of Nythe Road at GR 182860 appears to have been altered in some way - possibly converted to an embankment. Green Bridge may also have been converted to a fixed bridge (it was originally a wooden drawbridge) by this time. A contemporary account[69] states that it was a wooden bridge with railings, and only formed an access to the fields south of the canal. There was a bacon factory to the north, but there was no road approach to the bridge, only a grassy lane.

During the 1920s the remaining undeveloped land west of Drove Road was built up, and there was much ribbon development here and along Shrivenham Road[2]. Garrards expanded their factory in Newcastle Street in 1926[43]. H C Preater Ltd had by now taken over the Ford franchise from Skurrays (who moved to Old Town) and expanded the premises along Princes Street. The old mill now became more commonly known as "Preater's Mill"[12].

A late 1920s photograph (converted to a transparency) of Swindon Wharf (Gilling's Wharf) shows a single storey building on the site displaying the sign "H Gilling and Son. Factors for the British Oil and Cake Mills and Products"[21]. A later photograph (captioned 1930s) shows the same building, and the same sign, but the scene is now dominated by large signs advertising petrol[21].

The 1925 edition of the Ordnance Survey 6 inches to the mile map of Swindon (revised 1922) shows much the same detail as the 1923 3rd Edition of the 1/2500 series referred to earlier, but with one or two significant differences which are presumably further revisions incorporated as a result of later publication. These revisions show Wellington Street Bridge now converted to an embankment and the canal infilling extending all the way to the former site of Drove Road Bridge. Apparently some of the derelict barges at Swindon Wharf were left in position when the canal was filled in[29]. The map changes just described are consistent with the conversion date for Wellington Street Bridge of 1922/23 suggested earlier, and dates the extension of in-filling to Drove Road at 1922/24.

The canal manager's villa at Swindon Wharf was still used as a private residence up to 1936, with Churchward of the Great Western Railway being one of its last tenants[10]. The other buildings at the wharf were still in use in 1937 as a Corporation Depot[10].

* Filled in, circa 1986/87.

According to Liddiard[19] a recreation hut was erected on the filled-in canal in the centre of the town during the economic slump of the 30s to provide a place where the unemployed could undertake such jobs as boot and shoe repairing, etc. A 1979 letter in the Swindon Evening Advertiser[78] states that there were two such huts, which were obtained from a nearby Army Camp built during the 1914-18 war. Later, in the early 1950s, the huts were moved to the Civic offices site in Euclid Street, where they remain to this day.

A 1936 revision of Sheet XV1.1 of the 1/2500 Ordnance Survey map shows extensive filling in of the canal from Stratton Wharf Bridge (now called "Wharf Bridge") westwards to Nythe Road, beyond which marshy ground follows the line of the canal to Green Bridge, the last quarter of a mile being more waterlogged than the rest. Nythe Road Bridge and the small access bridge to the east appear to have been levelled but Green Bridge still stands. The track crossing the canal and shown leading to Nythe Farm on earlier maps has now become Nythe Road and leads to a sewage works.

The canal to the east of Stratton Wharf was still watered at this time.

Tapscott-Mason[52] states that the canal manager's house at Swindon Wharf was empty by 1939, with the rest of the site still in use as a Corporation Depot. The site was already earmarked for a new fire station, but World War II prevented this being built until the late 1950s. Mr Tapscott-Mason has some photographs of the site taken in July 1939. He also mentions that communal air raid shelters were being dug in the canal in-fill between Regent Street and the site of the junction with the North Wilts canal at this time.

Queenstown School was modernised in the same year[73].

The 1942 revision of sheet XV4 of the 1/2500 Ordnance Survey map shows the canal to be filled in from the centre of Swindon out as far as Drove Road. York Road and Whale Bridges are still shown. Swindon Wharf is still named as such, in spite of the basin being filled in. Sheet XV4 shows that the slopes at the rear of the towpath on the north side of York Road Bridge have now been converted to steps. This must have happened after 1939 because Tapscott-Mason sketched the bridge in July 1939, and the conversion had not taken place then[52]. Perhaps, and this is only speculation, there were air raid shelters on the canal site nearby, and the steps were constructed as a safety measure. Measurements of the map representation suggest that the steps on the east side were about twice as steep as those on the west side. However, the 1956 edition of the same map shows steps of equal length and steepness - whether this was a genuine alteration or a map error is difficult to say.

The RAF serial survey photographs taken in March 1948[88] show steps of equal length, so if there was a conversion of the eastern steps, this must have taken place between 1942 and 1948.

A transparency copied from a 1950s photograph of the former site of Drove Road Bridge is held in Swindon Museum[21] and shows a low embankment over which Drove Road passes. Several large culvert pipes run through the embankment on the line of the canal, and there appears to be some water immediately adjacent to the embankment, even though the grassy infill further away appears dry. The Walcot area to the east of the Drove Road was liable to flooding at this time[28]. The towpath on the northern "bank" runs up to Drove Road and appears to be tarmaced.

The RAF aerial surveys of 1946[89] and 1948[90] provide interesting information on the state of the canal and its environs at this time. Immediately east of Drove Road the canal is shown watered eastwards beneath Marsh Farm Bridge as far as the point of entry of the Coate Feeder (GR 167855), where the early 20s infill starts. At this point the reservoir referred to by R W May[69] is clearly visible*; this reservoir existed until 1986 at the rear of Radio Rentals*. At the western end of this reservoir a dam separates it from the rest of the canal. Just south of the reservoir the aqueduct carrying the Coate Feeder over the River Cole can be seen, and a storm run-off from the canal into the river is evident some 200 yds further west.

There are large areas of allotments both north and south of the canal on this section (those on the north side still exist), and the cleaner appearance of the canal both west and east of these allotments suggests that the gardeners found the canal a convenient dumping ground for weeds and garden rubbish.

Further east, the 1946 survey[91] shows the filled in canal in the vicinity of Green Bridge. From east of the reservoir, the infill appears very uneven and is grassed over, but the tow-path on the south bank and its adjacent hedgerow are well defined. The photograph is taken from too great a height to discern the detailed configuration of Green Bridge, but the lower level 1948 survey [92] provides more information. The sun on these photographs was shining from due west along the line of the canal, and the shadows of iron railings can be seen on the western side of the bridge. These railings continue round from the northern end of the bridge westwards along the north bank of the canal, dividing it from the entrance to the St Margaret Bacon Factory. No opening under the bridge is visible on the west side which may indicate that the infill of the canal was right up to bottom of the bridge, or that the bridge had by now been converted to an embankment. Details of the eastern side of the bridge are in shadow, but the shadows indicate that it is at higher level than the infill to the east, with the road approach from the north being embanked above the fields to the east. The rest of the scene is little different from the 1946 survey, except that a considerable length of the canal infill between the reservoir and Green Bridge appears to have been levelled and much of the southern hedgerow removed.

South of Green Bridge, the road turns into a track across fields. Hooper[42] states that Green Bridge was demolished about 1956/57. At this time he states that a stream ran along the line of the canal beneath the bridge. Although this stream is not visible on the aerial survey photographs this does not preclude its existence, and this would provide a reason for the retention of the steel guard rails. It seems likely on this evidence that the bridge had not been converted to an embankment when the aerial photographs were taken. In contrast to R W May's description of the bridge in the early 20's as a wooden bridge[69], Hooper remembers the bridge as a stone bridge at the time of demolition. It is therefore possible that the bridge was reconstructed between the 1920's and 1950's. It is not possible to settle this point from the aerial survey photographs.

Further east the 1946 aerial survey photographs[93] show the canal filled to within about 300 yds west of Stratton Wharf Bridge, as depicted on the 1936 Ordnance Survey map. Nythe Road Bridge has been levelled, and there is no trace of the smaller bridge to the east at GR 182860. The arch of the Stratton Wharf Bridge is clearly visible, but the canal appears to have been filled in immediately adjacent to the bridge to provide communication

* Filled in, circa 1986/87.

roads or tracks to Wharf Farm at the NW corner of the bridge. There is a track across the canal immediately west of the bridge, and another track appears to run beneath the bridge arch to a farm building east of the bridge. Since the bridge carried the busy A419 at this time the advantages of these tracks are obvious. Eastwards, the canal is watered for a considerable distance as the line veers towards the Oxford Road. A line of willows along the north bank - still present today even though the canal has been filled in - stands out. The watered sections on both sides of Stratton Wharf Bridge are shown as very weedy with only a few clear patches of water. This section of the canal was not covered by the 1948 aerial survey.

During the mid-50's a large sewer was laid along the line of the canal east of Queenstown Bridge towards Drove Road, in preparation for the development of the eastern side of Swindon in the early 60s. A serious fire occurred in the Garrards Factory just west of York Road Bridge on 21st March, 1958, destroying many new buildings constructed in the factory expansion of 1956. The factory was rebuilt, but following the virtual collapse of the company in the late 1970s, the factory was closed and has now been demolished. The 1956 Edition of the 25 inches to the mile Ordnance Survey maps show little change from the 1942 maps, apart from the representation of York Road Bridge steps, already referred to.

A series of photographs taken in 1957 of some of the former bridge sites is held by Swindon Reference Library. These show Whale Bridge, Preater's Mill and York Road Bridge still standing and looking much the same as they did when the canal was in use. The bed of the canal is now waste ground with a metalled footpath (the former towpath) on the north side. The steps of the converted slopes at the northern end of York Road Bridge are pretty shallow, as might be expected, since a slope as steep as a normal flight of steps would be virtually impassable to horse drawn traffic.

A transparency taken from a slightly later photograph of Preater's Mill and Whale Bridge, held by Swindon Museum[21], shows the tower of Preater's Mill to have the word "FORD" in large letters on each side of the tower, denoting the car agency held by the owners. The bed of the canal at this time was grassy and strewn with rubbish, with many old oil drums in evidence. A trickle of water runs down the northern side of the infill, near to the towpath. Cars parked nearby indicate that the photograph was taken in the late 1950s or early 1960s.

A 1957 photograph of the area adjoining the site of the junction with the North Wilts Canal shows a metalled car park which is indicated as such on the 1956 25 inch map. (In fact it had been used for this purpose since at least as early as 1937 - see Section I.) A copy of a 1960 photograph of the former site of Queenstown (Wellington Street) Bridge, converted to a transparency, is held in Swindon Museum collection[21]. The view is looking north across the bridge site from College Street towards Wellington Street, and shows the east side of the road marked off with posts. There is a low wall along the edge of the former towpath on the Wellington Street side, separating it from the lower level infill.

At some time in the late 1950s, the canal feeder from Coate was blocked off from the canal, and apart from the 70 yd long reservoir immediately adjacent to the end of the feeder, the canal was filled in for a further quarter of a mile westwards, towards Marsh Farm Bridge. These changes are shown on the 1959 1/2500 Ordnance Survey plan SU 1685, revised January 1958. The aqueduct over the River Cole is still shown, and the feeder is designated "Old Feeder". By the middle 1960s the aqueduct had been demolished and the feeder broken up, only scattered remnants remaining in the fields south of the river. These changes are shown on the 1964 edition of the 1/1250 plan SU 1685NE (revised March 1964) and the 1965 edition of plan SU 1685SE (revised February 1965).

During 1958/59 the old buildings on Swindon Wharf site were demolished to make way for a new fire station which was officially opened in October 1959. (The previous fire station was in Cromwell Street, and was demolished during the construction of the Brunel Centre in 1970.)

The early 1960s saw the beginnings of the extensive redevelopment of Swindon which has continued up to the present time, and is still continuing. The redevelopment associated with the Parade (1961-64) and Fleming Way (1963-65) have already been referred to in Section I. At the same time extensive industrial and housing development of the eastern part of Swindon south of the canal line and east of Drove Road took place, filling in the area between Drove Road and Ermin Street (A419) in the east. The estates constructed were the Nythe and Covingham housing estates, and the Greenbridge and Nythe industrial estates. The Greenbridge industrial estate and the Nythe housing estate were built right over the line of the old canal, covering the already filled in section from about 3/4 mile west of the former site of Green Bridge eastwards to the A419 and the site of Stratton Wharf. Here, the modern Trajan Road follows the canal line just west of the A419, and the short watered section west of Stratton Wharf Bridge must have been filled in during its construction. The watered section to the east of the A419 was filled in for a distance of about half a mile from Stratton Wharf Bridge eastwards in the mid 1960s with spoil from the construction of extensions to the Pressed Steel works[1]. These works are sited north west of Green Bridge at GR 169860, and were originally established in 1954[2]. It is probable that Stratton Wharf Bridge was demolished and levelled in the late 1950s or early 1960s. The 1969 revision of the Ordnance Survey 25 inches to the mile map, Sheet SU 1886/1986 shows that the bridge has gone, and also the extensive development just described.

Whale Bridge and York Road Bridge were still in use up to at least December 1962, on the evidence of photographs held by Swindon Reference Library. Preater's Mill was still in use in 1962 as a garage, but the old Cetus Buildings on the north bank of the canal just to the east of Whale Bridge had been demolished by this time[27], as had the "Whale" public house, which closed on 6th February, 1962[99].

An aerial photograph of the Whale Bridge area, taken in late 1962, is held by Messrs Walker-Jackson Ltd[44] who had taken over H C Preater Ltd in the same year. This shows an oblique low level view from just south of the canal, embracing the length from Queenstown School in the west to the Garrards factory in the east. Preater's Mill stands some 75 yds east of Whale Bridge, and the cleared area formerly occupied by Cetus Buildings is evident at the western end of Medgbury Road. The terraces of Lowestoft Street immediately south of Preater's Mill, since demolished, can also be seen.

The canal line to the east of Whale Bridge is mainly grassed, whereas a higher proportion of tarmac is apparent to the west.

Construction of Fleming Way (dual carriageway west of Whale Bridge and single carriageway east of it) necessitated the demolition of both Whale Bridge and York Road Bridge. This demolition almost certainly took place during the first year of construction, 1963.

Certainly Preater's Mill was demolished in 1963[44]. Photographs taken at the commencement of construction of Fleming Way, from the still standing Whale Bridge, are held by Messrs Walker-Jackson Ltd[44]. They show large piles of builder's rubble in position along the line of the canal, to be used to raise the level of the bed to that of Princes Street and Corporation Street, the streets on either side of Whale Bridge. No doubt this rubble came from the wholesale destruction of the old brick terraces in the area during redevelopment.

Apparently Whale Bridge was so soundly constructed that dynamite had to be used during demolition[45].

A photograph taken at the time is held by Swindon Local History Society and shows that the large Whale Bridge roundabout was built around the bridge before it was demolished. The view is from west of the bridge, and shows the bridge standing forlornly in the middle of the embryonic roundabout, the kerbstones of which are already in position. A portion of the northern approach to the bridge is also included within the roundabout. Such was the size of the roundabout that Nos 1 and 2 Medgbury Road, at the western end of Medgbury Road (part of the terrace built in the 1890s), also had to be demolished to make room for it.

An undated newspaper photograph held in Swindon Reference Library shows demolition of York Road Bridge in progress. Comparison of tracings taken from pre- and post-Fleming Way large scale maps shows that the new road occupies the whole width of the widened canal adjacent to York Road Bridge, and hence complete removal of the embanked southern approach which jutted out into the canal was necessary. The newspaper photograph does in fact show the southern embankment being demolished.

Whilst this demolition necessitated a complete rebuild of the southern abutment, the northern abutment remained relatively unaltered, the broad steps down to towpath level remaining to this day. Slight differences in the colour of the bricks below where the main span would have been suggest that the northern abutment was refaced here with either the original bricks or very closely matching ones. Original bricks may also have been used in the reconstruction of the southern abutment. The original coping stones used on the pillars at the ends of the bridge parapet also appear to have been replaced. Insofar as adjacent buildings are concerned, only the end house in York Road at the south east corner of the bridge has been demolished as a result of the reconstruction, and with it the adjacent steps down to the backs on the east side of York Road. These steps and the end house have been replaced by a broad paved slope of easy gradient providing pedestrian access from Fleming Way to York Road. The steps to the backs of York Road on the west side have been removed, the remaining slope paved, and access blocked off by a brick wall at York Road level. This brick wall is continuous with the parapet of the reconstructed abutment, and the brick facing of the abutment is continuous with the side wall of the slope on the eastern side, which implies that all of these alterations were carried out at the same time. To match the steps down to Fleming Way from Graham Street (north side), the slope leading up to York Road has the same type of iron railings set into coping stones on top of the side wall.

Whale Bridge was completely destroyed, and no visible trace of its existence remains. It is, however, commemorated in the name of "Whale Bridge" given to the large roundabout which now occupies the site, whilst the nearby filling station which now occupies the former site of Preater's Mill is called "Whale Bridge Filling Station" and is owned by Walker-Jackson Ltd. The filling station was opened in August 1965, at the same time as Fleming Way itself.

Comparisons of tracings taken from pre- and post-Fleming Way large scale 1/1250 (50 inches to the mile) maps show that the canal line occupies the southern carriageway west of Whale Bridge, and that the bridge itself was sited on the southern part of the roundabout, (as shown in the Swindon Local History Society photograph already described), where the two southern pedestrian subways emerge into the open space in the middle of the round-about. The "Whale" public house would have covered part of the eastern side of the round-about.

Comparison of the 1966 1/1250 plan of York Road Bridge with its 1956 equivalent, par-ticularly in regard to the number of steps on the converted slopes down to road level from the northern abutment, shows that the pavement was raised slightly during the construction of Fleming Way to above the level of the lower two or three steps. Wholesale demolitions occurred in 1967/68 in the vicinity of the Parade and along the south bank of the canal at the northern end of Princes Street, which was itself greatly increased in width to become a dual carriageway. Many new buildings including the Law Courts, the Wyvern Theatre, the Wiltshire Hotel and most recently the Nationwide Building Society headquarters, not to mention multi-storey car parks, have grown up where the old brick terraces used to be.

North of the canal the eastern end of Cheltenham Street (GR 151849) beyond its cross-ing of Fleet Street, and the southern end of Wellington Street were demolished to clear a space for a coach station and a new General Post Office. The latter opened in 1965. A slide in the Swindon Museum Collection[21] taken in 1967 shows the cleared site for the coach sta-tion, but construction had not yet begun.

The majority of these changes are shown on the 1966 1/1250 Ordnance Survey plans SU 1584 NW and NE (revised 1965). These plans also show a new roundabout on the former site of Drove Road Bridge, with Queens Drive - a new road opened in 1953[2] - leading from it. The 1969 revision of the Ordnance Survey 25 inches to the mile, Sheet SU 1685/1785 (revised 1967) shows the reservoir at the rear of Radio Rentals, now at the western end of the Greenbridge Industrial Estate. It is marked as "Pool" and is about 70 yds long at GR 166855 and is adjacent to the entry point of the Coate Feeder.

During 1971-73 the Wiltshire Hotel was built on the south side of Fleming Way, just west of Islington Street.

In the latter part of 1973 the last remaining watered section of the canal in eastern Swindon near Marsh Farm Bridge was culverted and filled in. A metalled footpath now runs along the canal line (see Fig. 22). Marsh Farm Bridge still stands, and apparently will be preserved as a public amenity[29].

Fig. 22: Marsh Farm Bridge, June 1991

Construction of a fourth pedestrian subway leading into Whale Bridge roundabout from Medgbury Road commenced in February 1975, cutting right below the old site of the "Whale" public house. The subway was opened in April 1976, and its creation involved the demolition of a further three houses (Nos 3, 4 and 5) at the western end of Medgbury Road.

In August 1976 a mural depicting the Golden Lion Bridge was painted on the end wall of the house in Medgbury Road nearest to Whale Bridge roundabout to commemorate the centenary of the birth of Alfred Williams, the Swindon writer, described more fully in the following section.

Construction of the Stratton St Margaret by-pass, a dual carriageway re-routing the A419 east of the village, started in 1976 and was completed in October 1977. This construction involved considerable alterations to the former site of Stratton Wharf Bridge, where the old route of the A419 (Ermin Street) was obliterated and replaced by a grassed area extending from the eastern end of Trajan Road to the edge of a link road to the by- pass some 100 yards or so further east. The by-pass itself is a further 150 yds beyond this, passing through what were formerly open fields, and crossing the section of canal filled in in the mid 1960s with spoil from the Pressed Steel Works.

Queenstown School was closed in the autumn of 1977 and converted to a Magistrates' Court, re-opening in its new role in July 1978[79].

In October 1981 the brick terraced houses on the southern side of Medgbury Road were demolished and have been replaced by flats for the elderly (Cockram Court).

The winter of 1984/85 saw the demolition of the Garrards Factory on the opposite side of Fleming Way. The site is now occupied by the B&Q DIY superstore and the adjacent Halfords store, with a large car park between these buildings and Fleming Way itself.

Further along the canal line at Greenbridge, the old bacon factory north of the canal was demolished in 1985 and replaced by the TEXAS DIY Store, which opened in the spring of 1986.

The use of Queenstown School as a magistrates Court ceased in 1990 and demolition commenced in March 1993. The intended future use of the site is not known to the author.

## PRESENT DAY EVIDENCE OF THE CANAL

Starting at the point on Fleming Way where it crosses the end of the Parade (GR 151849), just north of the former junction site, and going eastwards along it, the canal line is followed until the complex of mini-roundabouts near the County Ground is reached, a distance of about half a mile. The canal bed would have occupied the southern carriageway nearest to the Parade as far as Whale Bridge roundabout, whilst beyond it the single carriageway continuation follows the canal line exactly.

Queenstown Bridge (or Wellington Street Bridge as it was sometimes known) would have spanned the canal just opposite the entrance to Falcon House, the Allied Dunbar office building next to Debenhams on the south side of Fleming Way.

A view from the top storey of the Wiltshire Hotel looking eastwards along the canal line is shown in Fig. 23. This photograph was taken in April 1974. Dominating the immediate foregound is Whale Bridge roundabout with Queenstown School (built 1880) at bottom left. Whale Bridge itself would have stood where the two right hand pedestrian subways meet in the centre of the roundabout, bridging the gap between the lamp-post and the shrubbery on the right hand bank. Walker Jackson's Whale Bridge Filling Station, on the far right quadrant of the roundabout, stands on the site formerly occupied by Preater's Mill, demolished like Whale Bridge in the early 1960s when Fleming Way was built. Parallel and to the left of Fleming Way, the brick terraces of Medgbury Road represent old Swindon, with the grassed area nearest to the roundabout being the former site of Cetus Buildings, which, having been built in the 1840s, were amongst the oldest buildings in this part of Swindon when they were demolished in the 1960s.

This photograph was taken before the construction of the fourth subway from the end of Medgbury Road into Whale Bridge roundabout in 1975/76. This construction necessitated the demolition of the end three houses nearest to the roundabout on the left hand (northern) side of Medgbury road. In October 1981, the brick terrace on the right hand (southern) side of Medgbury Road was demolished to make way for the present day flats for the elderly, known as Cockram Court.

Beyond Whale Bridge Filling Station in the photograph is the Garrards factory (demolished 1984/85) and in the top right hand corner the tower of Swindon Fire Station marks the former location of Swindon Wharf, and Drove Road Bridge. In line with the end of Medgbury Road the tall stands of the County Ground, home of Swindon Town FC, can be seen in the middle distance.

The canal line bends in a more southerly direction beyond Garrards (as does Fleming Way) and some 50 yds afterwards the unmistakable site of York Road Bridge is reached. Unmistakable because the ends of the bridge remain to this day. The northern abutment (Graham Street side) still retains the side steps down to towpath level and apart from some refacing, appears virtually unaltered since the canal days (apart from the fact that the steps were slopes at the time the canal was in use). The southern abutment (York Road side) has been considerably altered, since an embanked approach used to stick out across the route of what is now the southern half of Fleming Way. A view of the northern abutment is shown

Fig.23: View East from Wiltshire Hotel along Canal Line, April 1974

in Fig. 24. The refacing where the span used to be can be seen from the differences in the colour of the brickwork and pointing.

Just beyond the bridge site on the northern verge of Fleming Way are some trees which are probably remnants of the hedgerow which used to line the canal towpath (see Fig. 20, p.56).

Fig. 24: Northern Abutment of York Road Bridge, April 1974

On reaching the end of Fleming Way at the "Magic Roundabout", the Fire Station on the southern side of the roundabout marks the former site of Swindon Wharf and Drove Road Bridge. The canal line becomes clearly evident again on the far side of Queen's Drive dual carriageway, immediately to the rear of the back gardens of Shrivenham Road, where widely spaced double hedges and a grassed area between with a tarmaced footpath lead up to Marsh Farm Bridge (see Fig. 22). Until the latter part of 1973 this section of the canal was still watered, albeit weed filled and dilapidated.

An aerial photograph of this section of the canal line is shown in Fig. 25, taken in 1963. The centre of the picture is dominated by the large roundabout, now converted to the complex of mini- roundabouts called the "Magic Roundabout", and beyond it is the County Ground. The canal line west (left) of the roundabout is indicated by the foundations of the new Fleming Way, still to be opened to traffic. In the bottom left of the picture the recently completed fire station (opened October 1959) stands out, with its tall practice tower. This is the former site of Swindon Wharf. Beyond the roundabout to the right (east) the watered section of canal leading to Marsh Farm Bridge (extreme right) can be seen, between double hedges.

Fig. 25: Aerial Photograph of the Canal Line near the County Ground, 1963 (Swindon Museum Collection)

In 1973 this watered section was culverted and filled in, and generally tidied up to give the pleasant walk that it is today. At the same time repairs were made to the parapets of Marsh Farm Bridge - the oldest canal bridge (1805) in Swindon today, and a present day reminder of the sturdy little stone arch bridges which characterised the Wilts and Berks Canal in Swindon during the last century. (Kingshill Road, the original Whale Bridge, Drove Road and Stratton Wharf bridges were similar stone arch bridges.)

Beyond the recently filled section, where the southern hedgerow finishes, the canal line was filled in much earlier, mostly before 1922. This infilling is now a rough and uneven area of waste ground, about a quarter of a mile long, leading up to the western edge of the Green bridge Industrial Estate. Here the canal line is higher than the ground to the south, which slopes down to the River Cole. Until the 1973 infilling, there was a storm run-off from the end of the watered section (at the end of the southern hedgerow) to the River Cole.

About 300 yard further on, the western edge of the Greenbridge industrial estate is reached.

The feeder from Coate used to enter the canal here, crossing the River Cole about 50 yds due south by an aqueduct. There is no trace (except possibly a few blocks of stone on the banks of the River Cole) of either the feeder or the aqueduct today, these having been demolished in the late 1950s/early 1960s. The path of the feeder is now underneath the western fringe of the industrial estate.

Beyond here the old canal is buried beneath the modern factories which form the industrial estate, although the line is marked intermittently by an old hedgerow which probably ran along the southern bank, and which in many cases forms the boundary between adjacent factories north and south of the canal line. This can be more clearly seen from the aerial photographs taken by Wiltshire County Council in the early 1970s and obtainable from Fairey Air Surveys Ltd.

At the eastern end of the industrial estate, the A361 heads due north over the railway. The former site of Green Bridge would be below the embankment which carries the A361 up to the railway bridge.

On the other side of the A361 the hedgerow continues, curving away in a south-easterly direction, as the southern boundary of the gardens at the back of the houses of Stonehurst Road. The ground falls away to the south here, which would have necessitated embanking the canal. A steepening of the gradient immediately adjacent to the hedge and the fact that the hedge itself keeps to a constant level is further evidence in support of the view that the hedge followed the southern or towpath side of the canal.

Some 200 yds further on the canal line passes beneath the Oxford Road (A420) into the Nythe housing estate, but the line may still be followed intermittently by various indicators. The old hedgerow that followed the towpath on the south side of the canal is next found on top of an embankment which separates the lower level back gardens of Weedon Road from the higher level gardens at the back of Haven Close, Juniper Close and Hackleton Rise to the north. Further east, between Nythe Road and Waverley Road (which run at right angles to the old canal line) the canal line is indicated by two isolated willow trees in the back gardens between the two roads. (Many more of these willow trees can be seen lining a watered section of the canal just east of the Stratton by-pass.)

Isolated bushes on the line continue to Trajan Road on the eastern edge of the Nythe estate, with this road being directly on the line of the canal.

The old route of the A419 (Ermin Street - a Roman Road) used to pass by the eastern end of Trajan Road, but with the opening of the Stratton by-pass in October 1977, the route was abandoned, and the former site is now grassed over. However, part of the old A419 remains just north of the grassed area, leading up to the White Hart public house. The intersection of the canal line with the old A419 road was the former site of Stratton Wharf and its bridge. Prior to the construction of the Stratton by-pass, the ruins of the old wharf buildings were still to be found on the east side of the bridge site. There was also a slight hump in the A419 at the bridge site, as a reminder of the embanked approaches needed for the stone arch bridge that used to be there.

All this was removed when the by-pass was built in 1976/77, but an isolated clump of four trees in the grassed area at the end of Trajan Road, in line with the northern side of the road, marks the former bridge site. These trees were, in pre-bypass days, adjacent to the eastern side of the bridge.

Between the end of Trajan Road and the by-pass, a slip road cuts across the grassed area to an access roundabout to the by-pass. The canal line is indicated by a line of trees between this slip road and the by-pass embankment, a line which continues on the other side of the by-pass along the northern boundary of the canal line.

Beyond the by-pass to the east, the canal line is much clearer, and is indicated by widely spaced double hedges leading after 200 yds or so to a well preserved watered section about 400 yds long. The section of the canal from Stratton Wharf Bridge to the start of this watered section was filled in the mid 1960s with spoil from the Pressed Steel works, when these works were expanded.

The watered section is worth a visit, if only to see the stony towpath on the southern bank and to see the canal in something like its 19th century setting, running through open fields, free from the accoutrements of the 20th century.

As mentioned earlier, in August 1976 a mural was painted on the end wall of the house in Medgbury Road nearest to Whale Bridge roundabout. The mural purports to show the Golden Lion Bridge in 1908, and was painted to commemorate the centenary of the birth of Alfred Williams, the Swindon writer and former railway worker. A general view of the mural is shown in Fig. 26.

The caption "Regent Street, 1908" is historically inaccurate (possibly owing to the mural being copied from a postcard view of the bridge with a 1908 postmark) since the raised footbridges shown in the mural were in fact removed in 1906, see page 26.

In 1991 the TOYS-R-US superstore was build to the east of the Stratton by-pass, just to the north of the watered section of the canal referred to above, which fortunately remains untouched.

Fig.26: Golden Lion Bridge Mural, Medgbury Road, September 1976

## SECTION III
## NORTH WILTS CANAL FROM ITS JUNCTION WITH THE WILTS AND BERKS CANAL IN SWINDON TO MOREDON
## (GRID REFERENCES 151849 TO 122873)

## HISTORY

The North Wilts Branch of the canal was built later than the main canal and was opened in April 1819[1]. In contrast to the main canal, which contained no locks in Swindon, the North Wilts Canal had to climb from the Thames Valley around Cricklade up to the junction with the main canal in Swindon. This necessitated a flight of three locks at Moredon, and a further flight of five locks at Rodbourne. There were also more locks between the Pry and Cricklade.

## 1814-1841

Construction of the North Wilts Canal began in 1814 but suffered delays owing to shortage of finance[1].

An 1820 hand drawn map at a scale of 20 inches to the mile is held by Swindon Reference Library, and has already been referred to in Section I, page 5. It was drawn by William McIlquham.

The various locks mentioned earlier are shown, together with the following bridges, in order northwards from the junction with the main canal: John Street Bridge (GR 150849); a bridge at GR 146852; a bridge near to the Lock House at Swindon Top Lock (GR 143856); Iffley Road Bridge (as it later became known) (GR 141857); Rodbourne Road Bridge (GR 138858); a bridge carrying a track to North Leaze (GR 133860); an access bridge at GR 125868, and Moredon Bridge (GR 122873).

Evidence from later paintings, maps and photographs suggests that the majority of these bridges were masonry arch bridges, the exceptions being Rodbourne Road Bridge, the bridge carrying the track to North Leaze, and possibly Moredon Bridge. However, it seems probable from present day appearance, and the fact that it carried a well used road to Purton, that Moredon Bridge was also a masonry (brick or stone) bridge of similar architecture to other canal bridges of the period. The bridge carrying the track to North Leaze at GR 133860 was probably a wooden drawbridge, whilst Rodbourne Road Bridge (known at the time as Telford Road Bridge) was a fixed steel bridge with trellis work sides[69]. Of the arch bridges, John Street Bridge (designated "Stone Bridge" on later Ordnance Survey maps) was definitely constructed from stone, and there is evidence to suggest that the next three bridges out to and including Iffley Road Bridge were also stone bridges. Moredon Road Bridge and the access bridge at GR 125868 may have been brick rather than stone. On the other sections of the main canal in Swindon, all the arch bridges were constructed from local stone (see Sections I and II), but on the North Wilts Branch, at some point in the northward progress of the canal, a change to brick construction took place, no doubt because clay became more readily available than stone in the Thames Valley. A brick arch bridge could be seen at GR 100918, about one mile due south of Cricklade (and about 5 miles from Swindon) until 1971, when it was levelled. The keystones from John Street Bridge, showing the date 1814, are held in Swindon Museum (thanks to the action of the then curator, Mr Gore, at the time the bridge was demolished in the 1920s).

The 1828 1st Edition of the Ordnance Survey 1 inch to the mile map[12] shows all the above bridges, but does not show the locks.

Virtually no building development took place in the vicinity of the canal until the arrival of the Great Western Railway in 1841.

## 1841-1914

The GWR line was opened from London to Bristol on 30th June, 1841[1] and crossed the North Wilts Canal at GR 147851. Swindon Station was opened in July 1842, whilst the railway works opened a year later in 1843[2].

In 1843, the canal owners made an agreement with the GWR to supply them with water, this being taken from the North Wilts Canal between noon on Saturdays and noon on Sundays[1]. At this time development in the vicinity of the canal was limited to one beerhouse (probably the forerunner of the Union Hotel) standing on the western bank where the canal passed under the Great Western Railway[2] just to the south of the railway.

By 1848 a short row of buildings on both sides of the canal had grown up near the beerhouse, near what was later the north end of Bridge Street[2]. These were known as Sheppard's cottages, taking their name from the owner of the fields in which they stood[2]. (The present day Sheppard Street runs through this area now, and it is believed that John Street and Harding Street were also named after John Harding Sheppard[52].)

The two 1849 paintings (see Fig. 2, p. 12) of Swindon held in the Railway Museum and Swindon Museum show the new railway works, the railway "village", the station, and about twelve buildings in the vicinity of the railway bridge over the canal consistent with the account in the Victoria County History of Wiltshire, Vol IX[2] given in the previous paragraph. The Swindon Museum painting shows four sets of railway lines crossing the bridge over the canal, but the angle of view does not permit the configuration of the bridge to be identified. However, the slightly different viewpoint of the painting in the Railway Museum shows that the canal passed through a stone arch beneath the railway, which ran along an embankment at this point.

Other features shown on the 1849 paintings are a wharf and one building on the northern side of the junction with the main canal; at the western end of the wharf is a stone arch bridge (later to be known as John Street Bridge) with a road or track running across it. The small bridge just north of the GWR bridge indicated on the 1820 and 1828 maps is also shown (GR 146852). It is depicted as a stone arch bridge, and appears to provide access between buildings on the east bank of the canal and a barn or cottage on the west bank. To the east of the small development in the vicinity of the railway bridge, open fields are shown. There is no sign of Sheppard Street or of what later became known as Bullen's Bridge (GR 148850).

A plan of the GWR works in 1846 is shown in Fig. 27. Note the small access bridge just north of the railway bridge across the canal and the reservoirs to the east, to which the canal provided water at weekends. These reservoirs provided the works with water by a syphon system, crossing the canal by pipe to that part of the works west of the canal[98]. The pipe itself ran beneath the railway bridge over the canal.

Fig. 27: Plan of GWR Works, 1846 (Alan S. Peck Collection)

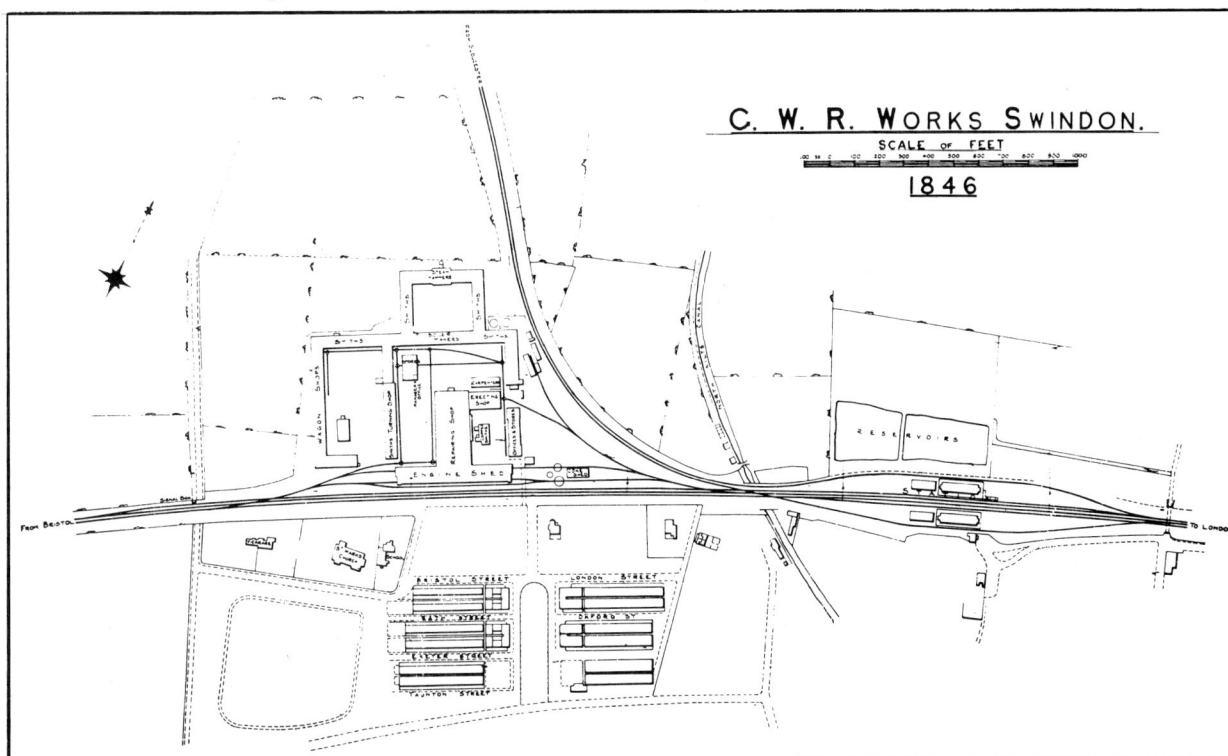

By 1851, the group of buildings adjacent to the canal in the vicinity of the railway bridge included the inns (or beerhouses) called "The Old Locomotive", "The Wholesome Barrel" and the "Union Railway Inn"[2]. Reference 99 provides more information on these three beerhouses.

The Union Tavern was opened in 1841 and was owned by J H Sheppard, who was also the brewer. In its early days it was also known as GWR House or Union Railway Hotel.

The Old Locomotive and the Wholesome Barrel were just north of the railway, also on the western bank like the Union Tavern, which was south of the railway. Both were owned by the Canal company. The Old Locomotive was the larger of the two, and was immediately adjacent to the stone arch bridge just north of the railway bridge. It opened some time prior to 1845 and may even have pre-dated the GWR.

The Wholesome Barrel was next door and to the north of the Old Locomotive. It appears to have been in use as a pub from 1841 until 1849. It then seems to have lain empty for a time and was let as a house in 1851 prior to demolition some time after 1854.

A drawing by J L Jefferies is reproduced in Reference 99, and is captioned "A scene on the North Wiltshire Canal, 1840s". It looks along the line of the canal to the south and shows the Wholesome Barrel in the foreground and the larger Old Locomotive in the background, immediately adjacent to the stone arch bridge. Through the arch of the bridge a second bridge can be seen a short distance further on. This must be the 1841 railway bridge which has vertical abutments with a shallow arch for the main span above them, as also shown in the 1849 painting described previously.

New Swindon in 1851 consisted of Westcott Place and Street, the railway estate, and the groups of houses adjoining the station, the Golden Lion, the Locomotive (Fleet Street), the Union Railway and the Whale[2]. The towpath ran right alongside the Union Railway and there was a special flagstoned area alongside the pub for the bargees to leave their horses[57].

Further development of the Bridge Street area occurred during the 1850s[2] and at some time during this period Sheppard Street was built and was carried across the canal at GR 148850 by an iron trellis bridge, which became known as the Union Canal Bridge (after the nearby public house) or Bullen's Bridge. According to Reference 8, the latter description arose from the name of the first licensee of the Union Tavern, the licensee being a Wantage man named Bullen. The bridge itself was said to be the first iron trellis bridge to be erected in Wiltshire, and had previously featured as an exhibit in the Great Exhibition of 1851[1]. It had been sent to the exhibition from the USA by the New York Iron Bridge Company, and was later purchased by Swindon Corporation[101]. From this it follows that the date of erection of the bridge in Swindon must have been about 1851/1852. A newspaper cutting dated "1950s" held by Swindon Reference Library, reproduces a painting of the bridge currently held by Swindon Museum. The painting itself is undated, and shows the iron trellis bridge as a flat span across stone abutments. The newspaper cutting also shows a modern photograph of Bridge Street and the description reads:

"The Old Union Canal Bridge - the first suspension bridge of the kind in Britain which joined what is now Station Road and Sheppard Street. Below is Bridge Street which has replaced the fields seen through the bridge to the right" (The view was from north of the bridge - Bridge Street was to the south.)

A handwritten comment alongside the reproduction of the painting is "1850s".

Dalby[9] considers that the bridge was not a true suspension bridge. The author is no expert on bridge engineering, and cannot therefore voice an opinion on this matter. Suffice it to say that the deck of the bridge was positioned a quarter of the way up the trellis work sides; a fact which probably has some significance in engineering terms. The span was high above the canal and the bridge approaches were embanked as they climbed up from street level (see Fig. 32).

The 1850 map of Swindon in Reference 8 shows development in the vicinity of the bridge, but there is no definite indication of the bridge itself. Other bridges which are shown on this map are John Street Bridge, and the railway bridge. The small bridge just north of the latter is not shown - presumably because it was not regarded as important enough, since it appears on later Ordnance Survey maps.

During the period 1851-61 the most important private development in New Swindon was the building of houses "along the lane from Eastcott to the end of Fleetway, and so north to the Union Railway Inn"[2]. North of the main canal, this development followed the line of Bridge Street, and was sporadic and confined to what were only workmen's cottages and beerhouses[2]. Other development took place between John Street, to the south of the canal at GR 149849, and the canal itself.

Between 1869 and 1877 200 houses were built on the north east side of the canal between the junction with the main canal and Station Road, forming the brick terraces of Gloucester, Cheltenham and Wellington Streets[2], since demolished during the 1980s redevelopment.

In 1872 the GWR was charged £100 for the right to widen their bridge over the canal.

Bullen's Bridge and the various other bridges mentioned were shown on the 2nd Edition of the one inch to the mile Ordnance Survey map of 1873/74[26].

The transfer of the canal from the Wilts and Berks Canal Navigation to the Wilts and Berks Canal Company in 1877 has already been described in Section I. The hand drawn map of the North Wilts Canal held by Swindon Reference Library, originally drawn in 1820 by William McIlquham, was almost certainly the one used in the conveyance of the canal to the new owners, since it is annotated "Conveyance from the Wilts and Berks Canal Navigation to the Wilts and Berks Canal Company, 15th March, 1877". Some idea of the state of the canal at this time may be gained from the pencilled comments on the map alongside the various locks and bridges. The bridge near to the lock house at Swindon top lock is noted as being "very bad". Iffley Road Bridge is "bad", whilst Swindon bottom lock to the west (at GR 136858) has the comment "walls need repairing, full of weeds". Several other locks are noted as being in need of repair, including the Moredon locks. It appears that the portion of the canal between the Moredon/Purton road bridge at GR 122873 and the Moredon lock-keepers house (GR 125871) was leased to the Midland and South Western Railway, because the comment is "For M&SWR railway July 6/1/77. Subject to right of way to cottage and lock along towing path". This railway was opened to Swindon in July 1881[47], and extended to Cirencester in 1883[64], crossing the canal at GR 123873.

The towpath was also used by railway workmen as a route from the villages west of Swindon (Purton, Shaw and Lydiard) to the Great Western works[35]. By joining the canal towpath just west of the Moredon/Purton road bridge and following it into Swindon, where it passed through the heart of the railway works, they were able to save themselves one and a half miles of walking. The need for this "short cut" disappeared when workmen's trains were introduced in the 1880s.

Two years earlier, in 1878, the great inconvenience caused by the lack of bridges over the two canals had prompted the New Swindon Local Board to give "£200 towards building a drawbridge in Fleet Street to avoid the detours of the old fixed bridges in Sheppard Street and John Street[2]. In fact, the reference to a drawbridge is misleading because Fleet Street Bridge (called New Bridge at the time) was built as a swing bridge. Details of its construction and mode of operation are given in plans held in the Wiltshire County Records Office[51], one of which has the date 10th July 1878. It was a steel girder bridge pivoting on a turntable on the east bank, at the Milford Street end of the bridge. The length of the swinging portion was 32 ft 10 in, some 19 ft of which overlaid the east bank. The canal width under the bridge was a narrow 12 ft, compared to 31 ft further away. 3 ft wide pavements are shown on each side of a roadway a mere 9 ft wide. A building at the north-west corner of the bridge is labelled "Stables", presumably for barge horses. The bridge was operated by a capstan at the north east corner. An undated painting of the bridge is held by Swindon Museum, and was reproduced in the Swindon Evening Advertiser in 1954[80] and shows the view looking across the bridge from the Fleet Street end towards Milford Street. Steel rails lining the sides of the bridge and the approaches are shown, and what appears to be a second capstan at the south east corner. The painting is virtually identical to a photograph taken in 1890, which is reproduced in Peter Sheldon's "Swindon in Camera"[60].

Fleet Street Bridge is shown on an 1882 painted map of Swindon held in Swindon Museum (Fig. 6, p.17), as are John Street Bridge, Bullen's Bridge, the GWR Bridge and the small bridge just north of it. Another painting dated 1880 shows "Telford Road Bridge", which later became known as Rodbourne Road Bridge. The bridge is depicted as a platform bridge with lattice work railings spanning the chamber of Swindon No 4 lock, just behind the lower lock gates, which were towards the eastern end of the lock chamber.

The new owners of the canal, as mentioned earlier in Section I, spent £17,000 on repairs, but all to no avail, and by 1882 tolls had fallen to £800.

A photograph of the Old Locomotive beerhouse situated just north of the railway bridge is reproduced in Reference 99 under the caption "The Old Locomotive, 1880s". The view is from the railway bridge (or the stone arch bridge) looking north over the pub at roof level. It is stated that the pub was sold to the GWR by the Canal Company in May 1888, together with land adjoining and then demolished.

The 1886 1st Edition of the 1/2500 (25.344 inches/mile) large scale Ordnance Survey maps and the even more detailed 10.56 ft to the mile plans of New Swindon of the same date provide much useful information on the canal and its environs at this time.

Sheet XV 421 of the 10.56 ft to the mile series (surveyed 1885) shows John Street Bridge, referred to as "Stone Bridge"; Fleet Street Bridge, referred to as "New Bridge", and a separate footbridge adjacent to it on the south side. This footbridge had steps up each side to a raised central span, so that it could be used when the main bridge had been swung to one side to allow barges to pass through. (It may also have been erected to allow the elimination of one or both of the pavements on the bridge itself, thereby allowing the roadway to be widened from the very narrow 9 ft.) These features are also shown on the smaller scale 1/2500 maps of the same date. A portion of sheet XV4 of this series illustrating these features is reproduced in Fig. 28, p. 82.

The continuation of the canal northwards is shown on the neighbouring Sheet XV416 and shows Bullen's Bridge (named as such) with an un-named public house at its northwest corner. This was almost certainly the Union Hotel. North of Bullen's Bridge the G W R bridge is shown widened to 11 tracks as compared to the 4 tracks shown on the 1849 painting. This widening probably occurred in 1872, after payment of £100 to the Canal Company as mentioned earlier. Stonework from the original 1841 bridge is still visible in the present day railway bridge, and measurements of the relative positions of the changes in stonework, brickwork and girder work in the bridge when matched to the 1886 map and later maps indicates that the original stone bridge was widened on its northern side only, using brick and girder work and not stone. The width of the bridge was increased from 49 ft to 146 ft.

This widening took the north face of the railway bridge to within about 50 ft of the small arch bridge just north of the railway, which had been there since the earliest days of the canal. The large scale map confirms the arch configuration of this bridge depicted on the 1849 painting of New Swindon, and in the J L Jefferies sketch[99].

The next sheet north, XV315, was the most northerly of the 10.56 ft to the mile coverage of New Swindon. Thereafter, the largest scale maps of 1886 vintage were those of the 1/2500 series (25.344 inches/mile) which do not of course provide such detailed information on bridge configuration as the large scale plans. Sheet XV315 shows the top two Swindon locks, the Lock House adjacent to the top lock on the east bank of the canal, and a bridge carrying a track from the west to it. The bridge itself is shown as an arch bridge, and is situated at the northern (lower level) end of the lock chamber, in other words at the opposite end to the lock gates. The approximate location of the top lock was GR 143856, and a widened section of canal stretched from its entrance to the gates of No 2 lock some 100 yds further up the canal. It is not possible to say without further evidence whether the bridge to the Lock House was constructed of stone or brick, but one local memory recalls it as a stone arch[24].

The smaller scale 1/2500 maps show the same features, but extend the coverage beyond the immediate vicinity of Swindon. In common with the larger scale plan XV315 just referred to, Sheet XV3 of the 1st Edition 1/2500 series (surveyed 1885) shows the canal passing through the railway works from Bullen's Bridge northwards, skirting the western fringe of a complex of sidings associated with Swindon Station. A large reservoir is shown just north of the latter. This was the GWR reservoir supplied with water from the canal at a charge of £250 per annum[1]. A gasworks is shown south of the canal at GR 140855. A portion of this map which includes the canal is shown in Fig. 29 (p. 83).

The gap between the No 2 lock and No 3 lock at Iffley Road is shown to be about the same, at 100 yds, as that between No 2 and the top lock. Again the intervening space is widened to permit waiting barges to pass each other, and to allow storage of water for operation of the locks.

No development is shown at the eastern end of Iffley Road adjacent to the canal and after its crossing of the canal at GR 141857 it becomes no more than a track across fields. The bridge is un-named and crosses the lower end of No 3 lock chamber (northern end). The scale of the map is insufficient to discern the configuration of Iffley Road Bridge, but confirmation that it was an arch bridge is provided by plans held by the County Records Office[51]. Two undated plans with the title "Swindon New Town Local Board - Private Street Improvements" give details of parcels of land being sold off at the eastern end of Iffley Road for development. One of the plans is a section along the centre line of Iffley Road, and shows a rise to the crest of the bridge of 11 ft compared with the road level at the western end of the road. The date of these plans must have been about the same as that of the Ordnance Survey map (1885/86) since the 2nd Edition of 1900 of the same sheet (XV3) shows that some development has taken place on the parcels of land that were up for sale. A former resident (now deceased) of Iffley Road, who used to live next to the bridge, has also confirmed that it was a stone arch bridge[69]. The same source also states that the lock keepers who used to live in the Lock House in the early 1900s were a Mr and Mrs Pope.

Beyond Iffley Road a widened section is shown between No 3 lock at Iffley Road and No 4 lock some 200 yds away at Telford (later Rodbourne) Road. The Telford Road crossing of the canal at GR 138858 is similar to that at Iffley Road in that the bridge crosses the lock chamber.

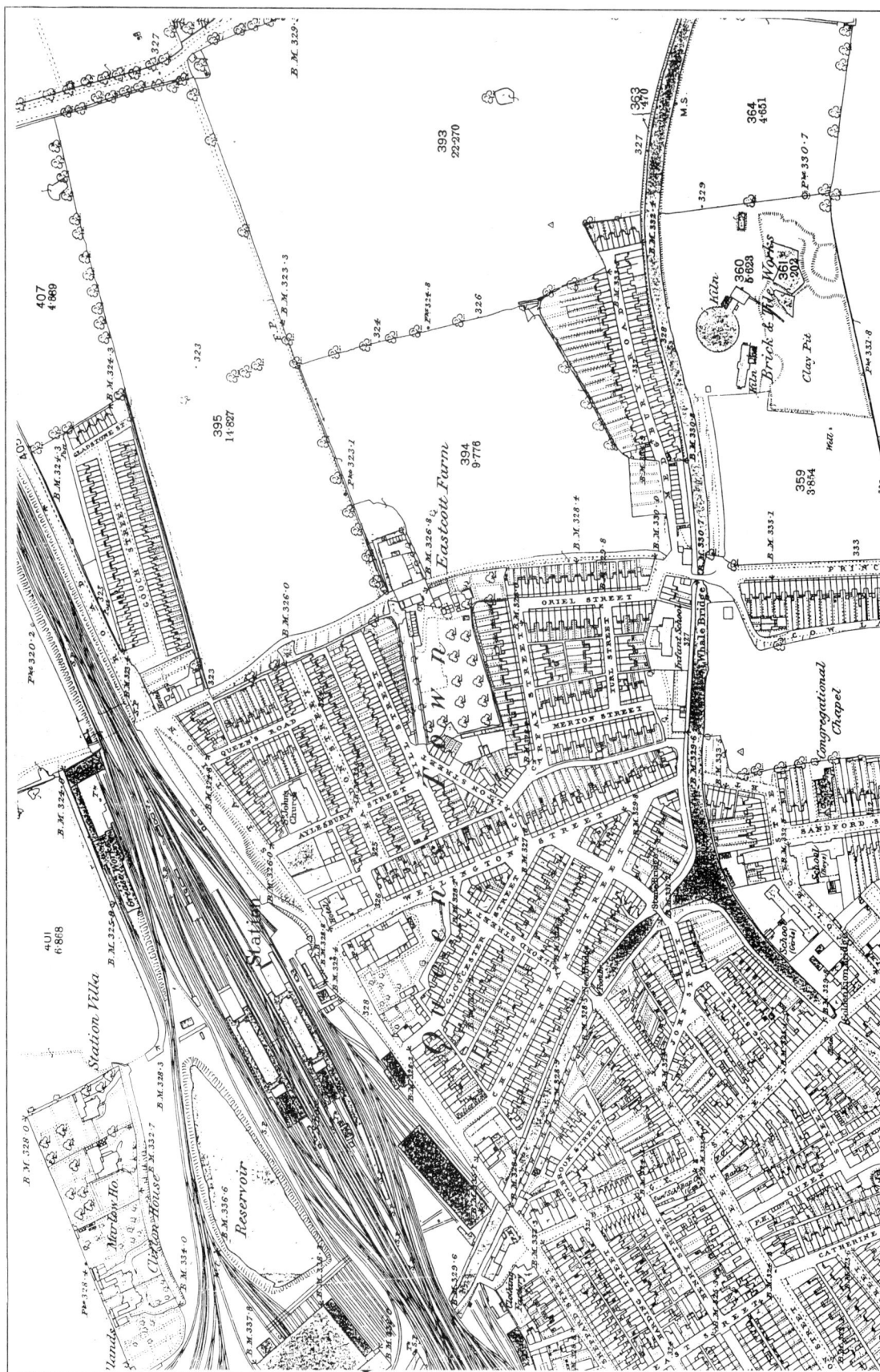

Fig. 28: A portion of Sheet XV4, Ordnance Survey 1/2500 Series, 1886 Edition (surveyed 1885) showing the Wilts and Berks Canal and the North Wilts Branch in Central Swindon

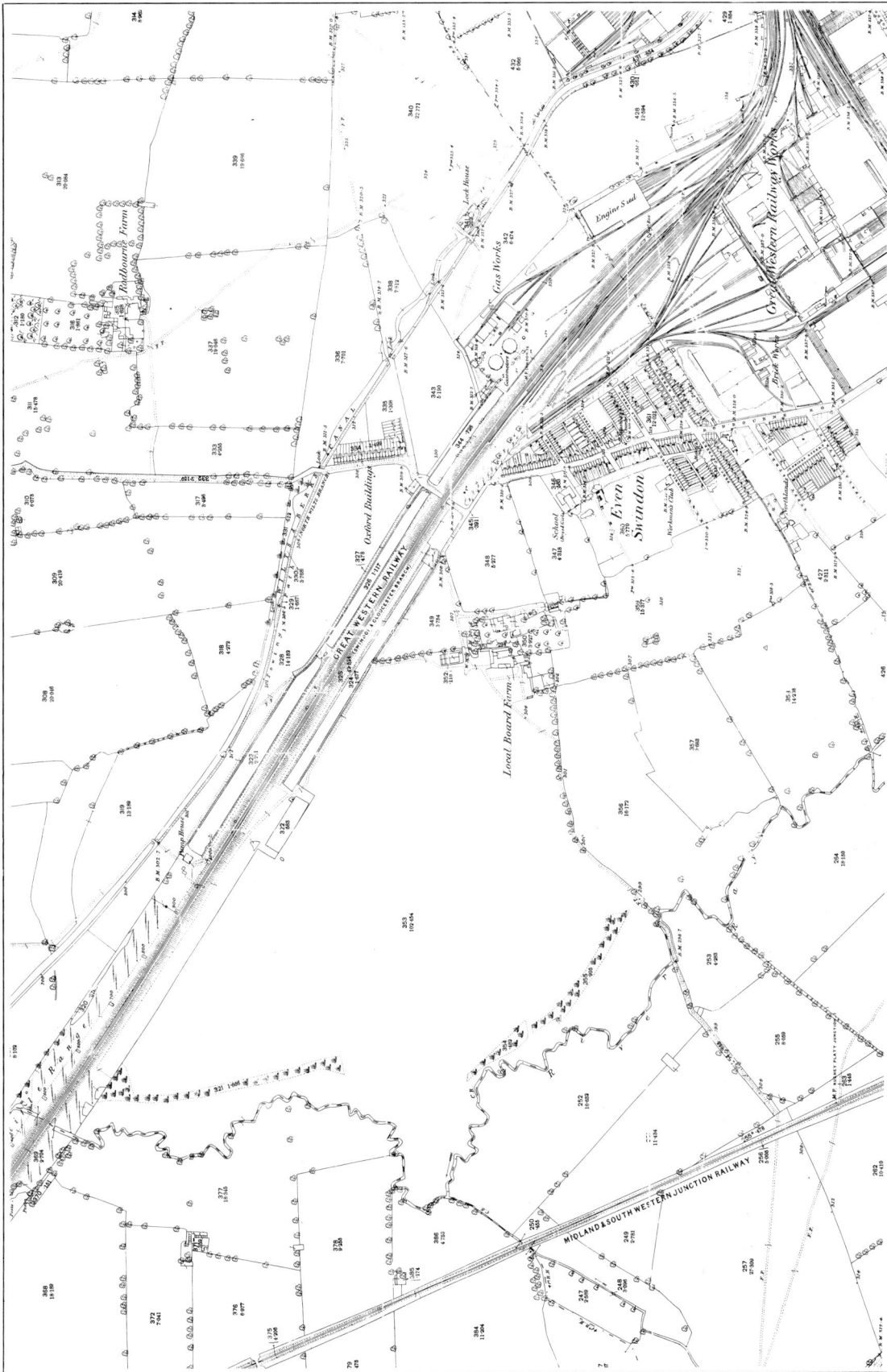

Fig. 29: A portion of Sheet XV3, Ordnance Survey 1/2500 series, 1886 edition (surveyed 1885), showing the North Wilts Canal through the GWR Works.

Immediately south of Telford Road Bridge, on the eastern side of Telford Road, a terrace of houses called "Oxford Buildings" is shown. These houses still exist today. A few houses are shown at the western end of Iffley Road next to Oxford Buildings, but no further development.

From here on the canal runs through open fields. Swindon bottom (No 5) lock is shown some 360 yds west of Telford Road at GR 136858. About a quarter of a mile further on a bridge carrying a track to North Leaze, a small settlement or farm north of the canal is shown (GR 133860). The towpath appears to go across the end of the bridge rather than underneath it, which would imply that the bridge was a drawbridge or a swing bridge, but it is not named as such. If it was a movable bridge, it was probably of wooden construction.

The canal follows a relatively straight path for a further half mile and then has to turn to a more northerly direction to follow the contours of a shallow valley formed by a tributary of the River Ray. The canal uses this valley to penetrate higher ground to the north (the line of the Purton/Blunsdon escarpment) and reach the Thames valley beyond it.

This northward section is shown on Sheet X15 (surveyed 1873/83) and an access bridge carrying footpaths from the west towards North Leaze in the east is shown at GR 12586. Surprisingly for such a minor bridge, it appears to be an arch bridge, and the canal towpath is shown passing beneath its western end. A possible reason for such anamalous treatment could be that it may have been used as the supply route to the Moredon Lock House which is shown on the west bank of the canal about 250 yds north of the bridge, adjacent to Moredon Top Lock.

Supporting evidence for this suggestion is provided by the present day appearance of the site, where there is clear evidence of an embanked approach (as would be necessary with an arch bridge) on the Western side, and also on the western side, a road or track alongside the canal running north from the bridge in the direction of the former site of the Lock House. The latter is noticeably separated from the lower ground to the west by an embanked western edge.

Between the top lock and Moredon No 2 lock, a widened section of the canal about 80 yds long is shown. Just beyond No 2 lock the canal crosses a stream which probably ran through a culvert since no aqueduct is indicated, and then immediately begins a sharp 90 degrees turn westwards to follow the valley.

Just short of the Moredon/Purton road, at GR 123873, the canal is shown passing under the Midland and South Western Junction Railway, opened in 1883[64]. The railway is carried on a low embankment at this point, and the bridge appears to be just wide enough to carry the single track - in all probability a simple steel girder platform on brick abutments.

Moredon Bridge is about 75 yds west of the railway bridge and the towpath is shown passing underneath its southern end, at GR 122873. It was probably a substantially constructed brick or stone bridge with a sloping span, since it had to carry the road up from the valley of the River Ray to the steeply rising ground north of the canal, the climb then continuing to a sharply humped brick bridge crossing the M&SW Railway.

Moredon Bottom lock was about 250 yds west of Moredon Bridge.

Whilst these large scale 1886 maps provide the earliest tangible evidence of the configuration of the bridges beyond Rodbourne, some 60 to 65 years after they were first built (all three were shown on the 1820 hand drawn map), it is more than likely that no major changes would have been made to them in this time because they were in open country and would not therefore be affected by the pressures resulting from new development.

In 1891 the charge made to the GWR for piping water from the canal was increased from £250 to £300 per annum, and in the same year the United Commercial Syndicate took over the running of the canal and spent £16,000 on dredging and lock repairs[1].

In spite of these efforts a trip on the canal in 1893 was not a very palatable experience according to a Mr Julius Auerbach, who described it thus[36]:

"The entrance to the North Wilts at Swindon is under an iron swing bridge, too low to pass under. (This would be Fleet Street Bridge.) A handle for this can be obtained at the adjoining public house. Just above this are the five Swindon locks, all close together, and for some distance the voyage is at times very disagreeable, owing to the foul stench of the mud stirred up by the oars. Apparently a good deal of sewage matter is somehow allowed to filter into the canal from Swindon. Several small swing bridges similar to those on the Wilts and Berks have to be raised during the trip" (to Latton and the junction with the Thames and Severn Canal).

The last sentence implies that Mr Auerbach used the term "swing bridge" to cover both swing bridges and drawbridges, but from the detailed description of Fleet Street Bridge it can be assumed that this was indeed a swing bridge.

As mentioned in Section II, amongst the plans held by the County Records Office[51] is a Swindon Corporation plan showing the level of the canal towpath between Rodbourne Road Bridge and Drove Road Bridge. The plan is dated April 1899 and shows the positions of Rodbourne Road Bridge (over lock No 4), Iffley Road Bridge (over lock No 3), No 2 lock, No 1 lock and the bridge to the Lock House, three GWR footbridges over the canal, the GWR railway bridge (labelled GWR subway), Bullens Bridge, Fleet Street Bridge, and John Street Bridge on the North Wilts and then Wellington Street Bridge, Whale Bridge and Drove Road Bridge on the main canal. The representation of the towpath between John Street Bridge and Wellington Street Bridge is of particular interest, since it is at a higher level than elsewhere, and there are noticeable additional "humps" in the immediate vicinity of the two bridges. Both of the bridges have embanked approaches, but photographs and maps show clearly that the towpath passed underneath the bridges, with no change in level, so the "humps" most probably represent slopes leading up to the bridge approaches to provide access to the streets, which of course would have to be included in the Corporation maintenance schedules for the towpath. These slopes are clearly visible in a 1914 photograph of John Street Bridge shown in Dalby's book[1] and are indicated on the large scale 10.56 ft to the mile 1886 OS plans (Sheet XV 8.1), but Wellington Street Bridge was not built at the time these plans were surveyed (1885). The 1914 photograph of John Street Bridge is reproduced in Fig. 30.

The higher level of the towpath between John Street and Wellington Street provides a pointer to the route taken by the barge horses proceeding from the North Wilts to the main canal east of the junction. Since the canal towpath west of the junction is along the southern bank of the North Wilts, and the towpath east of the junction is on the northern bank of the main canal, it would have been necessary to cross the canal from south to north at either Fleet Street Bridge or John Street Bridge.

Fig. 30: John Street Bridge, c 1914

The photograph of John Street Bridge in Fig. 30 is taken from Fleet Street Bridge and shows that there is a broad track on the north bank with a slope up to John Street Bridge, as well as the towpath on the opposite bank, so either could have been used by the barge horses. However, both track and towpath are at the same level, and so it is impossible to say whether the normal route involved crossing at Fleet Street Bridge or John Street Bridge, since the Fleet Street crossing would not be indicated by a change in level on the towpath plan, whereas that at John Street would be. The change in level at John Street would also be shown if the crossing to the north bank had already been made at Fleet Street. Perhaps both routes were used when approaching from the North Wilts direction, but for barges coming up the main canal from the south west, it would be more convenient to cross at John Street Bridge rather than go on further to Fleet Street. Certainly, the "official" towpath is designated on the OS plan immediately east of John Street Bridge on the north bank of the junction, whereas no towpath designation is shown on the north bank between Fleet Street and John Street. The OS plan shows slopes up to John Street Bridge from the canal on both sides and at both ends of the bridge, and the photograph already referred to shows the towpath on the southern bank passing beneath the bridge arch, whereas on the northern bank the track does not go under the arch, which comes right down to the water's edge.

The 2nd Edition of the 1/2500 series of Ordnance Survey maps, published in 1900, show only a few changes from the 1886 1st Edition described in detail earlier.

Between 1883 and 1898, the dates of survey of the 1st and 2nd Editions, Webb's timber yard was moved from the site near Cambria Bridge (see Section I) to a site on the west bank of the North Wilts Canal, immediately south of Bullen's Bridge.

Sheet XV4 (revised 1899) shows the footbridge on the south side of Fleet Street Bridge to have been removed, possibly because the canal was so little used by 1899 that the need for a separate footbridge had vanished. A photograph of Milford Street taken in 1890 is reproduced in Reference 97 and provides more precise dating for the removal of the footbridge. The view looks east across Fleet Street Bridge along Milford Street towards a shop entitled "Niblets Aerated Water Manufacturers". The footbridge to the south of the main bridge has gone. Since the footbridge was shown on the 1886 1st Edition of the 1/2500 series of maps, which were surveyed in 1885, it must have been removed between 1885 and 1890, assuming that the dating of the photograph of Milford Street is correct. Neither Fleet Street Bridge or John Street Bridge carry names on the 1900 map, but Bullen's Bridge is still named as such. Apparently the locals also used to refer to Bullen's Bridge as "Station Road Bridge" or "Cheltenham Street Bridge"[69]. Even more confusing, the railway bridge just to the north was also referred to locally as Bullen's Bridge and was referred to as such in the local press when reporting criminal incidents which occurred there[69]. As today, dark subways invite crime, and the sinister darkness beneath the bridge, with its narrow towpath and the added danger of the nearby canal, made it a place to be dreaded by day or night[69].

The Great Western Railway bridge over the canal is shown widened to its present day width, carrying 18 tracks as compared with the eleven shown on the 1886 1st Edition map. It must therefore have been widened at some date between 1885 and 1899, possibly in 1892 when the GWR made its final conversion from broad gauge to narrow gauge. An article in the Evening Advertiser of 20th November 1981[96], adds credence to this and quotes "Mr Harry Harper" in saying that large numbers of broad gauge locos were put to rest in the Railway Works extension at Rodbourne. A photo taken in the 1890s illustrates the article and shows dozens of locos crammed nose to tail at Rodbourne which is of course just west of the rail bridge over the canal. Many extra sidings were needed in Swindon whilst this operation was in progress[41]. Measurements of the changes in brickwork, stonework and girder work on the present day bridge show that this final widening occurred on both sides of the previous bridge, increasing the width from 146 feet to 351 feet, and in the process over-running the old arch bridge to the north - almost akin to a cuckoo in the nest!

Apparently to compensate for the loss of the arch bridge, a new footbridge appears a few yards north of the railway bridge, with steps leading up to it on the east bank of the canal and the span crossing directly to a higher level on the west bank. This bridge was one of three new footbridges erected across the canal to aid communication between parts of the GWR works, which had now expanded on both sides of the canal. The other two bridges appear on the neighbouring Sheet XV3 (revised 1899) at GR 145853 and GR 144855. The canal ran between high banks at these points and the bridges had no direct access to the canal towpath below. (The more southerly of these two bridges was not demolished until

October 1982. It was of steel construction with sheet steel sides - see Fig. 31.) The most northerly of the three bridges (GR 144855) was at the northern boundary of the works about 50 yards south of Swindon Top Lock. It carried a footpath to the open land on the east bank of the canal, just north of the works, designated "Recreation Ground" on the 1900 map. These three footbridges were also shown on the Corporation's 1899 plan, already described.

Fig. 31: GWR Footbridge over Station Road/Iffley Road Cycle Track/Footpath, March 1974

Iffley Road Bridge is now named as such, whilst the series of locks is called "Rodbourne Locks". Since the 1st Edition, new development has occurred on the south side of Iffley Road, but none on the north, and the eastern end of the road is still not built up. Telford Road has been renamed Rodbourne Road and Rodbourne Road Bridge is named.

Sheet X15 (revised 1899), covering the section beyond Rodbourne Road to Moredon, shows no changes from the 1886 1st Edition.

In 1900 Swindon New Town and Old Town joined to form one corporation, using as their headquarters the Town Hall which had been built at the foot of Victoria Hill in 1891[2]. By 1901 the population was 45,006; north of the railway the settlements of Even Swindon and Gorse Hill were extended especially in the Ferndale Road area[2]. The western end of Ferndale Road joins Rodbourne Road just north of Rodbourne Road Bridge.

The arrival of Kemble water in 1903 finally removed the need for the GWR to draw water from the North Wilts Canal, although at this time its ability to supply was very limited[98]. The two reservoirs north of the station were back filled in the early years of the century and when a large extension to the carriage brake shop was made in 1910, the south east corner brick foundations had to be set 29 feet deep to bed below the puddling of the pond[98].

Fleet Street Bridge was strengthened in 1904 prior to the opening of the new Swindon Tramway system in September of that year[6].

A photograph of Fleet Street Bridge showing a tramcar on the bridge is held by Swindon Reference Library, and is reproduced in Reference 6. The photograph is undated but was probably taken between 1904 and 1914. As indicated by the 2nd Edition (1900) of the 1/2500 Ordnance Survey map, Sheet XV4, the footbridge to the south of the main span has gone, although differences in the fencing shown in the photograph on the southern bank of the canal indicate where the footbridge was situated. The towpath on this bank is fenced off from the bridge at the road edge, blocking the path, indicating that the canal was no longer in use at the time.

Another photograph dated 1910 held by the Reference Library shows Rodbourne Road Bridge, the configuration being as depicted in the 1880 painting described earlier. The terraced houses of Oxford Buildings appear in the background. A transparency taken from a 1914 photograph of the bridge is held by Swindon Museum[21] and shows the view of the bridge from the west. The canal appears virtually dry and full of weeds, and a man is standing in what should have been the canal bed. The lock gates are still in place and partly open. The loss of water from the canal in 1906 following the collapse of the Stanley aqueduct caused certain parts of the North Wilts canal to become dry, as reported by the canal manager to the Parliamentary Committee in 1912[1] (p. 27).

A 1914 photograph of John Street Bridge is held by Swindon Reference Library and is reproduced in Fig. 30. The view is from Fleet Street Bridge and is remarkably clear.

## 1914 to the Present

In 1916, as part of the improvements to Swindon Tramways, Fleet Street Bridge was replaced by a solid embankment[6].

Following the Swindon Corporation Closure Act in 1914, and the cessation of hostilities in the Great War in 1918, filling in of the canal began in the early 1920s[19]. Plans related to this activity are held in the County Records Office[51] and have already been referred to in Sections I and II. Insofar as the North Wilts canal is concerned, plans in the numbered sequence dated February 1920 show the intention to convert John Street Bridge, Bullens Bridge and Rodbourne Road Bridge into embankments and to make improvements to the already converted Fleet Street embankment. In all cases the embanked bridge approaches were to be lowered, the roadway widened and, in the case of Rodbourne Road, straightened. The canal was shown watered at all four sites. Fleet Street embankment was to be widened from 15 ft 3 in (the width of the original bridge) to 30 ft. Another plan of the Fleet Street embankment, dated 18th February 1920, shows a section along the centre line in which a dotted line below the surface is labelled "Top of pipe", indicating that the embankment was culverted. A later plan of the conversion of Bullens Bridge is annotated "Copy to TC 2nd January 1923. Previous copy in possession of Town Clerk dated May 1922". This shows the canal to be filled to within about 9ft of the south side of the bridge, but watered thereafter. Evidence from the 1/2500 1923 OS map (see below) confirms that this infilling was done before 1922, and since the earlier 1920 plan of Bullens Bridge showed no infilling, this puts the date of infilling at about 1920/21.

Sheet XV4 of the 1923 3rd Edition of the 1/2500 (25.344 inches to the mile) Ordnance Survey maps shows the canal to have been filled in from the junction with the main canal as far as Bullen's Bridge by the revision date of the map - 1922. John Street Bridge has gone - the crossing is shown by the dotted lines, but apparently the raised approaches were still present as late as 1939[10]. Fleet Street Bridge is shown as an embankment (see above) but Bullen's Bridge is still shown. The latter agrees with the annotations on the later plan of the Bullen's Bridge conversion described in the previous paragraph, which make it clear that the Town Council had not acted on the conversion proposal by January 1923, well after the 1922 revision date of the OS map. From here to just north of the railway, the canal is shown watered and is marked "Canal (Disused)".

What appears to be a dam across the canal is shown at the northern end of this section, immediately north of the footbridge erected when the railway bridge was widened (GR 146852). North of this dam, and continuing on Sheet XV3 (revised 1922), the canal through the Railway works appears to have been partially filled on the eastern side, leaving a narrow strip of water alongside the towpath on the western bank. The second footbridge at GR 145853 is shown, but the third footbridge on the northern boundary of the works (GR 144855) has been replaced by an embankment. A short watered section then follows to the northern end of the top lock, but thereafter to Iffley Road the canal has been completely filled and has railway sidings running over the former line. Whilst the Lock House remains, its bridge, Iffley Road Bridge and No 2 and No 3 locks have all gone. It seems likely that this section was filled in by the GWR between 1920 and 1922, because a 1920 map of the railway works in Reference 98 shows the locks and Iffley Road Bridge still untouched. No plans for the conversion of Iffley Road Bridge to the embankment shown on the 1923 Ordnance Survey map are included in the Borough council's collection of plans (vintage 1920) for bridge conversions in the borough[51], and this omission may imply that the conversion was delegated to the GWR.

A description of access to the western side of the bridge to the Lock House from the blocked off towpath about this time has been provided by R W May[69]. In a sketch plan accompanying this description May shows the towpath blocked off from Iffley Road just north of the western end of the bridge, and a spiral ramp constructed from bricks leading from it up to the embanked approach to the bridge (one went under the bridge on the towpath and the ramp then curved back towards the northern side of the bridge approach, thereby economising on space). The area immediately north and west of the terminated towpath is marked "GWR Factory". The canal is still shown watered, with the lock gates in position, so this may have been the situation in the intervening period between the acquisition of the land by the GWR, and the commencement of infilling and the construction of the sidings. The Lock House Bridge provided an access to the rear of the GWR works and to the Rodbourne Recreation Ground.

Beyond Iffley Road (which has been widened and straightened at the former bridge site), there is a short watered section to No. 4 lock, which had been filled during the conversion of Rodbourne Road Bridge to an embankment. The filling extends to just short of the bottom lock, and then resumes just west of it to about 350 yards west of Rodbourne Road. Thereafter the canal remains watered and little changed from the situation shown on the 1900 maps (continuation westwards on Sheet X15 - revised 1922). The only change appears to be the conversion of the former M&SWR bridge at GR 123873 into an embankment.

The only photograph the author has been able to trace of Bullen's Bridge, dated 1923, in the form of a transparency, is held by Swindon Museum[21]. This is reproduced in Fig. 32. It is a most informative photograph and appears to have been taken at the time the bridge was being dismantled and the embankments levelled. The photograph confirms the configuration of the bridge depicted in the 1850s painting referred to earlier, and shows that the bridge was much higher up than the present road, and this must have necessitated steeply embanked approaches. In the photograph the new road is being constructed at canal level just south of the bridge, where the filled in section to the junction begins. There is a "Road Closed" notice on the towpath and piles of road making materials beneath the bridge. The end of the watered section beneath the Railway Bridge can be seen in the foreground.

The date of this photograph, 1923, corresponds with the date suggested by Mr E Pullen for the demolition of Bullen's Bridge[37], and also with the evidence of the plans held in the County Records Office[51] described earlier. Mr Pullen was employed at Webb's timber yard adjacent to the bridge at the time, and states that the local unemployed were used to do the job. He has some memory of the bridge span being taken to the Town Gardens (in Old Town) afterwards, but there is no trace of it there now, and the author has been unable to confirm this suggestion. According to Mr Pullen, the canal was filled from Bullen's Bridge to the junction (and beyond as far as Queenstown Bridge) in 1921, and the part at the rear of Cheltenham Street, between Bullen's Bridge and Fleet Street, was then used as allotments. This again agrees with the evidence of the Corporation plans for the Bullen's Bridge conversion.

In 1925 the growing demands of Swindon for electricity caused a search for a site for a new generating station to be made, to replace the inadequate one built to supply the tramways (originally built in 1903). A site at Moredon was chosen (GR 124874). Quoting from Dalby's account[6] "... The abandoned canal leading to Swindon would provide facilities for the disposal of ash and laying of cables. An area of eleven acres and the whole length of the canal and towing path to Swindon, seven acres, was purchased from Pembroke College, Oxford for £1,200." The new power station opened in 1929, on the north bank of the canal just to the east of the Moredon/Purton road bridge. It had two wooden cooling towers and two more were added in 1930.

Fig. 32: Bullen's Bridge, 1923 (Swindon Museum Collection)

According to Harber[24], the GWR gas works SW of Iffley Road was extended about 1927, and the present day gasometer built on the line of the canal immediately south of the former site of No 3 lock and Iffley Road Bridge. This expansion entailed removal of some of the railway sidings which formerly occupied the site.

A further edition of the 1/2500 Ordnance Survey maps should have appeared in the late 30s, but publication was only partially completed when World War II started, and the coverage of the Swindon area by the 1936 revision is incomplete. Only Sheet XVI.I covering the Green Bridge/Stratton Wharf section was issued after the 1936 revision; the remaining sheets being issued after the 1942 revision. There is thus a 20 year gap in map information relating to the canal, and this 1922-1942 period is the one which is least documented, and for which the author would welcome information from readers.

At some time during the period the present day cycle track from Station Road was built, mainly for the use of workers in the GWR works. It used the canal towpath from Station Road (site of Bullen's Bridge) to the northern end of the partially filled section (GR 144855), by the former site of the top locks. (The present day continuation to Iffley Road, which deviates east of the canal line, came later.) Typical of the fallibility of human memory, one source[24] states that the canal alongside of the cycle track was filled in 1930-33, whilst another source[38] states that it was still watered in 1935/36! The first source[24] believes that the Lock House adjacent to the former site of Swindon Top Lock was demolished in 1926. It was however shown on the 1925 Ordnance Survey 6 inches to the mile map[10], and this map also shows the canal to be completely filled in all the way from Station Road to Iffley Road, discounting what was said earlier about this being done in the 1930s.

The GWR sidings between Iffley Road and the former site of the top lock had been removed by 1933, and the cycle track extended to Iffley Road on its present day route. This is shown on a 1933 Street Map of Swindon, which is reproduced in the Swindon Museum slide collection[21]. The map is too diagrammatic to resolve the uncertainty about infilling discussed in the previous paragraph.

All of the changes mentioned in the preceding paragraphs are shown on the 1942 revision of Sheet XV3 of the 1/2500 Ordnance Survey maps. The canal is shown filled all the way to Iffley Road, and all locks and the Lock House have gone. The watered section between Iffley Road and Rodbourne Road remains, but the filling from Rodbourne Road westwards is now continuous to the former site of the bridge carrying the track to North Leaze (GR 133860), a distance of some 650 yds from Rodbourne Road. The bridge itself has gone, but the canal remains watered west of this. A building has been erected on the line of the canal just east of the former site of Rodbourne Road Bridge. A site visit confirmed that this was a bungalow at the rear of the modern filling station present on Rodbourne Road at what would have been the eastern side of the canal bridge. (The filling station has been subjected to much alteration during the late 70s/early 80s and during the course of these alterations the bungalow has been demolished.)

The gasometer on the canal line just south of Iffley Road is also shown.

Sheet XV4, which covers central Swindon, also revised in 1942, surprisingly still names the Sheppard Street/Station Road crossing of the canal as Bullen's Bridge. The canal is shown filled, corresponding with the northward continuation on Sheet XV3, and the cycle track is named as such. The footbridge erected in the late 19th century just north of the railway bridge has gone.

Sheet X15, revised 1941, covers the section from west of the former site of North Leaze bridge to beyond the Purton/Moredon road bridge. The canal is still shown watered or marshy to the southern boundary of the power station, with all bridges, locks and the Moredon Lock House being shown. The short section within the power station boundary has been filled in, but the canal is watered west of the railway embankment. The Moredon road bridge now appears to have been converted to an embankment. Apparently one of the lock gates at Moredon top lock was still in position in 1939[52].

In 1942 Moredon Power Station was expanded to provide increased generating capacity, the filled in section of the canal forming part of a coal stockyard. A new concrete cooling tower was built in 1946 to supplement the existing wooden cooling towers[8].

In the same year, the RAF conducted an aerial survey of the area, and in so far as the canal is concerned, the situation shown by the aerial photographs is little different from that depicted on the 1942 OS maps[94]. The short watered section between Iffley Road and Rodbourne Road has now been filled in, but there has been no new infilling further west, and the canal is watered all the way to Moredon Power Station from just west of the former access bridge at GR 133860. The photograph does not extend quite as far as the Power

Station, but shows the top two Moredon locks and the Lock House, together with the bridge at GR 125868. The altitude is too great to permit details of this bridge to be discerned. The chambers of the two locks appear to contain water, but the length between the two lock chambers may have been filled in.

A further aerial survey two years later, in 1948, was carried out at a lower altitude and shows more detail[95]. The 1946 cooling tower at the Power Station stands out, and the lock chambers have been filled in. Otherwise the scene is little different from 1946, with the canal being watered south of the locks, although the bridge at GR 125868 may have been converted to an embankment by now (if it was not already an embankment in 1946). The Lock House still stands, and a large reservoir has been created north west of it, south of the Power Station. A water channel leading in the direction of Moredon No 2 lock from the reservoir may imply that the canal (which is at a higher level than the surrounding fields here) was drained to create the reservoir.

The next large scale maps of the area to be issued were the 1958 series of 1/2500 plans. Plans SU 1386 and SU 1287, both revised in 1957, show the section from West of the Rodbourne Industrial Estate to Moredon, and the canal is now completely filled in all the way to the Power Station. The two upper Moredon locks and the lock house have gone, together with the access bridge at GR 125868, but the short section between the railway line and Moredon road bridge is still watered. According to one source, the canal was filled and the lock house demolished in the 1940s[29]. Since the lock house was still intact and the canal still watered in March 1948, as indicated by the RAF aerial survey[95], this statement, if true, implies that demolition of the lock house and filling of the canal must have occurred between 1948 and 1950. Brickwork of the top lock chamber is still visible today beside the filled in canal.

Sheet SU 1385 (revised 1956) shows the beginnings of the Rodbourne Industrial Estate being built over the canal line. Work started on this estate in 1955, but by the time the map was drawn, the southwest corner of the estate was still undeveloped, with the road network being indicated by dotted lines. The road leading into the estate from Rodbourne Road follows the canal line exactly for a distance of about 200 yds westwards. Just on the western fringe of the estate a short section of the canal about 150 yds long remains unfilled.

In 1958, the old Union Hotel at Bullen's Bridge was demolished[99]. A photograph of the old pub was reproduced in the Swindon Evening Advertiser in 1975[39]. It was purchased prior to demolition by the owners of the neighbouring clothing factory (Compton Sons & Webb) in order to permit factory extension on the site[99]. The GWR gas works was demolished in 1959, apart from the Iffley Road gasometer, which remains to this day[24].

The old Midland and South Western Junction Railway which crossed the canal at Moredon was closed to passenger traffic in 1961[47].

As mentioned in Sections I and II, between 1961 and 1964 extensive redevelopment of the area surrounding the site of the junction with the main canal took place. South and west of the junction, the houses in the streets bordering the canal were demolished from beyond Regent Street on the main canal round to Fleet Street on the North Wilts branch. They were replaced by the shopping precinct of the Parade, and associated multi-storey car parks. North of the junction, the whole triangle of terraces bounded by Milford Street on the west,

Wellington Street on the east and the canal line on the south, was demolished to make way for the new Head Post Office and coach station.

The Rodbourne Cheney Industrial Estate was completed in 1964[2], and by 1967 the Hreod Burna Senior High School had been built north of the canal at GR 128868. The 1969 revision of the 25 inch to the mile Ordnance Survey plans, sheet SU1286/1386, shows these changes and it can be seen that the school playing field encroaches on the line of the old canal along its southern boundary, with the boundary fence following the towpath on what was the southern bank of the canal.

The short watered section west of the industrial estate is also shown. This has in fact been cleaned out for use as a reservoir and for angling, and lies west of the former site of North Leaze bridge at GR 129863.

As mentioned in the previous sections, the section of the canal line between Fleet Street and the junction with the main canal became the western end of Fleming Way during 1963/65. Redevelopment continued south of Fleming Way between the Parade and Fleet Street, and in January 1970 the large office block AEU House was opened at the corner of Fleming Way and Fleet Street at what would have been the south east corner of Fleet Street Bridge.

In April 1973 Moredon Power Station ceased generating electricity, and demolition began in the following year. The wooden cooling towers erected in the 1920s were demolished in August 1974, and the remnants of the coal stockyard and its overhead distribution gantry were demolished in February 1976. Finally, in 1979, the area lost two of its most noticeable landmarks when the concrete cooling tower and the tall concrete chimney, built in 1946, were blown up. The cooling tower was the first to go, on 1st March, and the chimney followed on 25th July. Photographs of these demolitions were reproduced in the Swindon Evening Advertiser on these dates. The power station site has now been cleared and developed as a housing estate (in 1991).

With the contraction of Swindon's railway works over the past twenty years, much of the former GWR estate has been demolished and the area north of the main Bristol line cleared for new building. West of the canal line is the new Hawksworth Industrial Estate, whilst east of it there are more factories, the North Star Technical College and the Oasis Leisure Centre. The grounds of the Oasis (opened on 1st January, 1976) border the cycle track and footpath which follow the canal line just north of the railway bridge.

The construction of Swindon's new northern distributor road began in 1978. This sweeps round the north western part of Swindon from the A3102 roundabout at Mannington, crossing the line of the old canal about 130 yds south of Iffley Road at a point which would have been mid-way between No 2 lock and No 1 (top) lock. This construction reached the canal line in the early part of 1979, and the cycle track and footpath were diverted slightly east of the previous line to go beneath the new road via an underpass.

Also in 1978, the construction was started of another new road linking the Hawksworth Industrial Estate on the west of the cycle track/footpath with the factories, the Oasis and the Technical College on the east side. This road is now in use, and crosses the canal line over a new bridge about a quarter of a mile south of Iffley Road. At this point the canal was in a cutting, now occupied by the present day cycle track and footpath, thus necessitating the bridge to carry the link road across it. This is a perfect example of how, even now, the old canal is still exerting an influence on the development of Swindon, some 70 years after it was closed.

Pedestrian access from the canal level footpath to the new road is provided by steps situated at the south east corner of the bridge. The bridge itself is of reinforced concrete construction with brick parapets - see Fig. 33 - and its position is about 60 yards south east of the former site of the most northerly of the GWR footbridges erected ion the 1890s (GR 144855).

Over the last decade, all of the brick terraces of Cheltenham Street and Gloucester Street to the north of Milford Street have been demolished and replaced by office blocks and a new road network. The western side of Cheltenham Street was the last to go in the early 1980s. Compton's clothing factory has also gone, and the site is now a car park.

During the late 1970s and early 1980s a rubbish dump was created south of the short watered section of the canal just east of Moredon Road Bridge (GR 123873) and in 1981 the rubbish dump began to encroach on the canal itself. This process has continued and the canal has now been completely filled in.

Fig. 33: New Bridge over Station Road/Iffley Road Cycle Track/Footpath, June 1991

In 1982, the old footbridge across the Station Road to Iffley Road cycle track (shown in Fig. 31) was demolished and the eastern bank of the canal cutting has since been converted to a grassy bank with all fencing and brickwork removed, to form the western edge of the Oasis leisure centre complex.

In 1984 the few remaining houses of Gloucester Street and Wellington Street south east of Milford Street and to the north of the bus station were demolished to make way for a new coach station and multi-storey car park, which were built over the period 1988/89.

Further office buildings (Tri-Centre Two) have been built on this site during 1989/1990.

The old railway bridge on the Purton/Moredon road just west of the Moredon Power Station site (which used to cross the Midland and South West Junction railway) was demolished and a new length of level road build alongside it in August 1988.

# PRESENT DAY EVIDENCE OF THE CANAL

Starting from the site of the former junction with the main canal just south of the pedestrian subway beneath Fleming Way (GR 151849) the line of the North Wilts Canal runs north west towards Fleet Street about 130 yds away. For the last 75 yds of this distance, the canal line is directly beneath the west bound carriageway of Fleming Way. Fig. 19, p.46, shows a view of the site of the junction from the top of the Head Post Office north of Fleming Way, and as stated in Section I, the centre of the junction would have been where the bicycle park is, between Debenhams (then Bon Marche) on the left and Primark (then Fine Fare) on the right of Fig. 19. Superimposition of Ordnance Survey large scale maps of different dates shows that John Street Bridge would have spanned the flower beds between Fine Fare (Primark) and the southern side of Fleming Way, about 60 yds west of the subway entrance. These flower beds are hidden from view in Fig. 19, but note the widened section of pavement on the far side of Fleming Way at the extreme right, and the lamp-post with a mushroom top just to the left. The northern end of John Street Bridge would have been where the lamp-post is - the foot of the lamp-post is in fact in a flower bed. The southern end of the bridge would be inside Fine Fare! The widened pavement has three seats upon it, not visible in Fig. 19.

Where Fleming Way meets Fleet Street, the former site of Fleet Street Bridge is where the traffic island is in the centre of the junction. The canal line continues as a projection of the line of Fleming Way across the traffic island to the start of the cycle track/footpath in Station Road that goes under the railway on its way to Rodbourne. Until the demolition of Cheltenham Street, the line was clearly recognisable as the back alley to the western side of the street. However the wholesale redevelopment that has now taken place has completely obliterated all trace of the line.

A photograph taken from the seventh floor of the AUEW building at the junction of Fleming Way and Fleet Street is shown in Fig. 34, and this was taken in May 1972, well before the demolition of Cheltenham Street. The canal line goes across the car park in the foreground, and along the back alley between the back gardens of Cheltenham Street on the right and the two storey factory building on the left. Looking further along this line, the entrance to the subway for the cycle track/footpath under the railway, which is directly on the canal line can be seen (just to the left of the six gable ends of the factory buildings). The canal line continues into the far distance with the Iffley Road gasometer and Moredon Power Station chimney and cooling tower acting as markers.

The former site of Bullen's Bridge is where the Rodbourne (Iffley Road) cycle track/footpath leaves Station Road. This bridge had a high embanked approach, and there is still a pronounced hump in the road at the site, most noticeable from the south-western side. The bridge itself would have occupied the northern carriageway of Station Road closest to the railway, since the southern carriageway was constructed behind the bridge when it was levelled in 1923, thereby allowing traffic to proceed whilst levelling was taking place, and eventually providing the wider road of today.

Fig. 34: View North from AUEW Building, May 1972

Fig. 35, taken in May 1972, shows the view looking northwest along the cycle track/footpath from where Bullen's Bridge used to be. The railway bridge under which the cycle track passes was first built in 1841 and subsequently widened in 1872 and again before the end of the 19th century. Since this photograph was taken, the factory buildings on both sides of the cycle track have been demolished, to be replaced by car parks and their associated entrances. However, the railway bridge itself has remained untouched. The present day frontage is that resulting from the late 19th century widening but, if one carefully examines the walls of the subway as one passes through it, a change from brick to stone some 20 yds inside the subway indicates the remains of the original 1841 bridge. The stone work lasts for just under 50 ft and the brickwork resumes again. Just over 32 yds from the further end of the stonework, a change in the brick and girder work indicates the limit of the 1872 widening, which was all on the northern side of the bridge. (The final widening occurred on both sides of the bridge.) At least the present day lighting alleviates to some extent the dread of attack that used to deter passage beneath the bridge in the days at the beginning of the century.

Fig. 35: Start of Cycle Track/Footpath from Station Road to Iffley Road, May 1972

The canal curved in a more northerly direction beyond the railway, between high banks as indicated by the high brick wall on the western side of the cycle track. (The eastern bank used to be similar but has recently been landscaped into a gradual slope and grassed over.) The towpath would have been on the same side as the brick wall. Many of the old railway buildings on both sides of the canal here have been demolished in recent years to make way for the new Hawksworth Industrial Estate on the western side and the Oasis Leisure Centre complex on the eastern side (opened January 1976).

About 200 yds beyond the railway bridge, midway along a short straight, there existed until October 1982 one of the old footbridges erected by the GWR across the canal in the late 19th century. This bridge is illustrated in Fig. 31, p. 88, taken in 1974. Three such bridges were erected to aid communication within the works, but this was the only one which persisted into the post war years. The others were sited just north of the railway bridge, and just round the bend of the canal indicated by the line of the cycle track in the background of Fig. 31. The remaining footbridge was demolished in October 1982, but the remains of the sawn off girders can still be seen on the top of the high brick wall on the western side of the cycle track, at the bottom of the wooden fencing.

Just beyond the bend is the newest bridge over the "canal", which was built in 1979. This bridge is shown in Fig 33 (p. 96). The view is from the south side of the bridge. This bridge carries a link road from the Hawksworth Industrial Estate on the left over the canal line to the Oasis and other buildings to the east of the canal. The new bridge is about 60 yds south east of the former site of the most northerly of the three GWR footbridges, which was demolished at some date between 1914 and 1922.

Just beyond this, the cycle track and footpath emerge from the deep cutting formerly occupied by the canal, and as the land drops away to the north, the cycle track/footpath diverges slightly from the line of the old canal to by-pass Iffley Road gasometer which is on the line. Further divergence from the line occurred in 1981 with the construction of an underpass beneath Great Western Way, a new northern distributor road to by-pass the town centre. The underpass takes the cycle track/footpath in a loop further east of the canal line, before rejoining the original path line north of the underpass.

Where the cycle track straightens out and starts a gradual descent towards Iffley Road is the start of the Rodbourne Locks section of the old canal. Between here and Iffley Road were the three top locks of the flight of five. Beside the top lock on the east bank was the lock house, reached by a stone arch bridge from the west bank of the canal (the towpath side). Because of the divergence of the cycle track east of the canal line, the former site of the top lock and the lock house is to the left (west) of the present day cycle track, about 150 yds from where the track starts to go downhill. The site of No 2 lock would have been just beyond the gasometer where there is a noticeable hump in Iffley Road today. This is all that remains of the embanked bridge approaches that were levelled when the bridge was demolished and the canal filled in during the period 1920-22.

Beyond Iffley Road the canal line procceds NW across an area of waste ground across which a footpath behind the back gardens of Iffley Road and Wembley Street leading to the Esso filling station in Rodbourne Road is on the line of the old canal towpath, which was on the south western bank of the canal here. The hedgerow adjoining the footpath probably dates from the days of the canal. If one looks back from Rodbourne Road along this footpath, the fact that the gasometer is directly on the canal line becomes immediately apparent.

The former site of Rodbourne Road Bridge and No 4 lock (demolished 1921/22) would be where the footpath meets Rodbourne Road.

The road into the Rodbourne Cheney Industrial Estate from Rodbourne Road follows the canal line for the first 200 yds, but from hereon the canal line runs on a more southerly course than the road, passing beneath various factory frontages before emerging again on the far side of the estate at the rear of Messrs Shorko Films Ltd* about two thirds of a mile from Rodbourne Road. No 4 lock was under Rodbourne Road Bridge, whilst No 5 (bottom) lock was about 260 yds west of Rodbourne Road, somewhere beneath the frontage to Raychem Ltd.

About a quarter of a mile further on the primary road through the industrial estate makes a right angled turn north, with a subsidiary road, Darby Close, branching off left. The branch road picks up the canal line again when it straightens out in a westerly direction and about 100 yds after leaving the primary road a spot corresponding to the former site of the bridge carrying the track to North Leaze is reached, in front of the GEC visitors car park at its western end.

Fig. 36: Cleared Out Section of Canal at the Rear of Shorko Films Ltd, Rodbourne Industrial Estate, March 1972

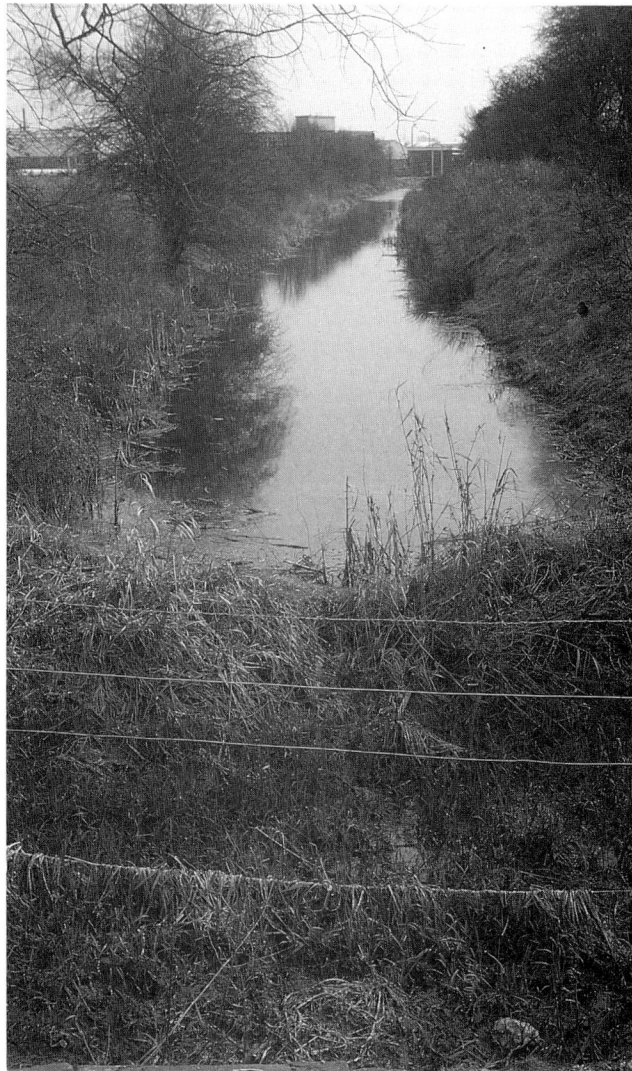

* Now called Courtaulds Films Shorko

No trace of this bridge remains today, and eventually the road comes to the entrance of Shorko Films Ltd beyond which a 200 yd stretch of the canal has been cleared out for use as a reservoir and for angling. This stretch is shown in Fig. 36, viewed from the western end. The buildings of the industrial estate can be seen in the background. This cleared out section is much deeper than the original canal, being about 18 ft in depth and originally finished 100 yds short of the western boundary fence of Shorko Films, but was extended right up to the fence in 1971.

Beyond this reservoir the canal line is clearly indicated by a footpath along the southern boundary of the playing fields of Hreod Burna School, which turns into a track between double hedges leading up to the former site of Moredon Power Station. The total distance from the end of the reservoir to the power station site is about three quarters of a mile.

The footpath past Hreod Burna playing fields is on the line of the canal towpath, which was on the southern bank of the canal. For most of this section the canal was embanked on its southern side to maintain the level above the shallow valley of a tributary of the River Ray immediately to the south. The hedgerows are probably survivors from the canal days.

About 350 yds beyond the school playing fields the track becomes less cluttered up with random bushes and the hedgerow on the south western side gives way to a fence as a cross track is approached. The cross track is on the site of a former arch bridge which probably provided a supply route to Moredon Lock House 260 yds further on, on the west bank of the canal. The remains of the embanked approach to the bridge can be seen in the field west of the canal line, and from it a stretch of level ground runs along the hedgerow adjoining the canal line northwards. This is raised slightly above the rest of the field, which slopes downhill to the west, and is probably the remains of the track to Moredon Lock House. A limited excavation should confirm the point. The bridge and lock house were demolished at some time between 1948 and 1957.

Near to the power station site, the track which follows the canal line has an ash surface. There is nothing remaining of the lock house which used to be situated near Moredon top lock, but some brickwork of the chamber of the top lock can still be found alongside the track.

No trace of the middle Moredon lock about 80 yds further on remains; a concrete service road to an electrical sub-station now covers the site. The former site of Moredon Lock House is where this road turns sharply westwards to go between two neighbouring compounds of transformers, just at the northern end of the remains of the top lock.

The line of the old canal is lost within the power station, but it would lie under the former site of the coal stockyard, on the southern (lowest) part of the power station site.* The canal made a sharp turn of over 90 degrees to a direction just south of west within the confines of the power station and was crossed by the M&SWR railway (the old Swindon/ Cricklade/Cirencester line) on the western side of the power station stockyard, which used

---

* The power station site has now been developed as a housing estate, known as Pembroke Park - after the former owners of the site, Pembroke College, who sold it to Swindon Corporation in 1925. Development commenced in 1991 and is still in progress (March 1993).

the line for its supplies of coal. The railway bridge was converted to an embankment soon after the canal was closed in 1914, but now the railway is no longer in use (it was closed to passenger traffic in 1961) and neither is the power station which closed in 1973 and was demolished over the period 1974-79.

Beyond the railway embankment, there is a rubbish dump which now covers a section of the canal which remained watered until 1981. This watered section ran between the railway embankment and the Purton/Moredon road. Encroachment of the rubbish dump began in 1981 and by April 1982 only 20 yds of the canal next to the railway embankment remained unfilled. This has since been filled in.

The road bridge was converted to the present day embankment at some time between 1922 and 1941. (The adjacent bridge over the railway was demolished and levelled in August 1988.)

Beyond this road the canal is watered in the winter, but tends to dry out in the summer. The line is clearly visible and about 250 yds west of the road the brickwork of Moredon bottom lock can still be found in the dry season, very overgrown by bushes. Further on there are many more relics of the old North Wilts Canal which can be found on its way to join the similarly abandoned Thames and Severn Canal at Latton.

## THE FUTURE

There is no doubt that there is a strong revival of interest in the local history and archaeology of Swindon, with particular emphasis on the recent past.

This interest has always existed within the local historical and archaeological societies with their committed membership, but perhaps more importantly for the future preservation and/or documentation of Swindon's industrial archaeology is the stimulation of interest amongst the general public. That this has happened is due not only to the efforts of these societies, but to many others, for example, the staff of Swindon Museum and Reference Library. The benevolent attitude of Thamesdown Council towards the old canal, as evidenced by the restoration of the old canal milestone to Canal Walk, the Jubilee Golden Lion nearby, and the tasteful restoration of the canal line in the vicinity of Marsh Farm Bridge, has helped greatly. However, the greatest influence has undoubtedly been the publication in the Swindon Evening Advertiser and the Wiltshire Star of the "Then and Now" series, and analogous articles, which reach a very wide section of the general public. Well presented and very readable publications like Peter Sheldon's "Swindon in Camera" and Michael Howell's "Bygone Swindon" can amplify the interest created by such articles.

The formation in the late 1970s of preservation groups for the canal (the Wilts and Berks Canal Amenity Group) and the former Midland and South West Junction Railway line (the Swindon and Cricklade Railway Society) are indicative of this re-awakened interest, and it is to be hoped that the future prospects for these two monuments to Swindon's industrial revolution will be better than the immediate past.

The WBAG has already greatly improved the watered section of the canal at Kingshill and the recent initiative by the staff and pupils at Moredon Junior School to tidy up the section of the North Wilts Canal west of the Purton/Moredon road has attracted sponsorship from Shell and Allied Hambro, now Allied Dunbar, and assistance and labour from the Manpower Services Commission. Such work can only enhance our appreciation of the efforts of those navvies of 180 years ago which were the trigger to the development of modern Swindon.

## TABLE ONE
## BRIDGES OVER THE WILTS AND BERKS CANAL AND THE NORTH WILTS BRANCH IN THE SWINDON AREA 1803 - 1993

## SECTION ONE
## WILTS AND BERKS CANAL FROM THE SOUTH WESTERN OUTSKIRTS OF SWINDON TO THE FORMER JUNCTION WITH THE NORTH WILTS BRANCH

1.     No name

| | |
|---|---|
| Grid Reference: | 137835 |
| Erected: | 1883 |
| Modified: | - |
| Demolished: | Still exists |
| Type: | Brick arch railway bridge |
| Dimensions: | Arch span - 34'6"<br>Width - 16'<br>Length of parapets - N side: 49'7"<br>                        S side: 43'2" |
| Remarks: | Single arch of elegant design built to carry the Swindon, Marlborough and Andover Railway (later known as the Midland and South Western Junction Railway) en route to Cirencester from Swindon Old Town station. The single track line was closed in 1961. Crosses canal line at a skew. |

2.     Sometimes known as Rushey Platt Bridge in the canal's early days

| | |
|---|---|
| Grid Reference: | 138838 |
| Erected: | 1803 |
| | Partially demolished before 1883.  Later footbridge across abutments (see below). |
| Type: | Wooden drawbridge (probably) over brick abutments. |
| Dimensions: | Not known |
| Remarks: | Access bridge to farm buildings at Okus. Span removed before 1883 but abutments left. Tracks from South and West Leaze met canal here. |
| Modified: | 1914-18 (probably).  Footbridge erected. |
| Demolished: | 1942-46 |

| | |
|---|---|
| Type: | Footbridge erected across abutments. |
| Dimensions: | Not known |
| Remarks: | Footpath provided a short cut up the hill to where the Princess Margaret Hospital stands today. No trace of the bridge remains today. Canal still watered from just south of railway bridge(1) to beyond this site towards Kingshill Road. |

### 3.    Kingshill Road Bridge (also known as Rushey Platt Bridge)

| | |
|---|---|
| Grid Reference: | 141840 |
| Erected: | 1803 |
| Modified: | - |
| Demolished: | 1920-22 |
| Type: | Stone arch road bridge |
| Dimensions: | Arch span - 18' (probably) <br> Width - 19' <br> Length of parapets - about 44-47' (probably) |
| Remarks: | Originally carried turnpike road to Wootton Bassett and first called Rushey Platt Bridge. Demolished during infilling in 1920-22, when embanked approaches were levelled, and the road straightened and widened. Site indicated today by a slight hump in the road. |

### 4.    Marlborough Street/Joseph Street Footbridge

| | |
|---|---|
| Grid Reference: | 143843 |
| Erected: | 1898 |
| Modified: | - |
| Demolished: | 1920-22 |
| Type: | Steel footbridge with steps up to raised central span. Sheet steel sides. Brick abutments. |
| Dimensions: | Span - 47' Width - 6' |
| Remarks: | Erected by Swindon Corporation. Demolished during infilling 1920-22. Today the site is marked by the roadway linking the two streets. The canal line is filled and grassed, and the former towpath is the tarmaced footpath on the Marlborough Street side which runs from Kingshill Road to Milton Road. |

### 5.    Cambria Bridge

| | |
|---|---|
| Grid Reference: | 145843 |

| | |
|---|---|
| Erected: | 1877 |
| Modified: | 1893 and 1978 |
| Demolished: | Still exists |
| Type: | Original bridge was steel girder bridge with steel side railings on brick abutments. 1893 bridge was a steel girder bridge with sheet steel sides on brick abutments. 1978 bridge is a reinforced concrete platform with steel side rails on original brick abutments. |
| Dimensions: | 1877 span - 18'<br>1877 width - 22'<br>1893 span - 17'9"<br>1893 width - 34'<br>1978 unchanged |
| Remarks: | First bridge built in 1877 by James Hilton, a speculative builder. A wharf for Webb's timber yard was situated just south of the bridge on the eastern bank. Widened and strengthened in 1893 by Swindon New Town Local Board at a cost of £1500. Due to corrosion, the main span was replaced in 1978 (by Thamesdown Council) by a reinforced concrete span with brick parapets surmounted by steel railings. The original brick abutments were retained, and the protective iron plate on the corner of the northern abutment (towpath side) shows characteristic rope wear grooves. Today the canal line beneath the bridge is filled, and continues as the footpath from Kingshill Road to Milton Road. |

## 6.    Black Bridge

| | |
|---|---|
| Grid Reference: | Slightly west of 147845 |
| Erected: | 1803/04 |
| Modified: | Before 1885 |
| Demolished: | 1885 - 90 |
| Type: | Original probably a wooden swing bridge. converted to fixed bridge before 1885, with brick or stone abutments and flat platform span with side rails. Gate at southern end. |
| Dimensions: | Not known for original bridge. Fixed bridge span (est) 18' Fixed bridge width (est) 12' |
| Remarks: | Converted to fixed bridge with embanked approaches at some time before 1885. Provided access to farm at foot of Eastcott Hill. The abutments of the fixed bridge jutted out onto canal to reduce the span required. Demolished 1885-90 during the development of the Rollestone Estate and replaced by Commercial Road Bridge 60 yds east. No trace remains today. |

7.    Commercial Road Bridge (Milton Road Bridge)

| | |
|---|---|
| Grid Reference: | 147845 |
| Erected: | 1890 |
| Modified: | 1981 |
| Demolished: | Still exists |
| Type: | Brick arch road bridge, originally with stone balustrades but in 1981 these replaced by concrete and brick balustrades. |
| Dimensions: | Arch span - 18'<br>Width - 45'<br>Length of parapets - 50' 3" |
| Remarks: | Replaced Black Bridge and sited 60 yds east of it. A wharf was situated on the south bank just east of the bridge just beyond the Central Club building (now demolished). Steps and slopes down to canal level removed at some time before 1960 and access from Milton Road fenced off. In 1977, steps at the NW corner were rebuilt to provide access to the Brunel Centre. Footpath from this subway to Kingshill Road passes beneath the bridge. Both frontages of the brick arch given an extra skin of new bricks in April 1981 and the old stone balustrades removed and replaced by concrete block and brick balustrades. |

8.    Golden Lion Bridge (Regent Street)

| | |
|---|---|
| Grid Reference: | 150847 |
| Erected: | 1804/06 |
| Modified: | 1870, 1877, 1898/1904, 1904, 1906 |
| Demolished: | 1918 |
| Type: | Original probably a wooden drawbridge. Replaced in 1870 by iron lift bridge. Raised footbridge added 1877 on NE side. Another footbridge was added on the opposite side between 1898 and 1904. |
| Dimensions: | Original bridge not known. 1877 bridge span 11', width 15' |
| Remarks: | 1870 bridge built and maintained by GWR. Roadway section raised by a vertical lift using chains in four end pillars operating against counter-weights. 1904 strengthened for new tramways. 1906 raised footbridges removed and level pavements added at sides of main span. 1918 replaced by solid embankment. |
| | Took its name from nearby pub with Golden Lion effigy on roof. No trace remains today. Canal line and site occupied by modern shopping precinct. New Golden Lion effigy erected near site in 1978 to commemorate the Queen's Silver Jubilee. |

9.      No name

| | |
|---|---|
| Grid Reference: | 149847 |
| Erected: | 1976 |
| Modified: | - |
| Demolished: | Still exists |
| Type: | Steel girder road bridge with sheet steel sides. |
| Dimensions: | Not known |
| Remarks: | Access bridge linking the vehicle unloading area on the roof of the Brunel Centre (Stage 1) with the later Murray John Tower complex. Does not really count as a canal bridge, hence not given a number (see footnote). |

## Notes on the Brunel Centre/Murray John Tower Complex

The Brunel Centre/Murray John Tower Bridge is not considered to be a true canal bridge because it's purpose is to bridge a gap between two neighbouring buildings rather than to bridge the canal or its remains. The canal line beneath the bridge was already filled in and paved over before the construction of the bridge, and it had no influence on the siting of the bridge. This is in contrast to the new bridge (no. 26) over the Station Road to Iffley Road cycle track/footpath, built in 1978/79, the need for which arose from the presence of the cutting created by the North Wilts Canal.

## SECTION TWO
## WILTS AND BERKS CANAL FROM THE FORMER JUNCTION WITH THE NORTH WILTS BRANCH TO THE EASTERN OUTSKIRTS OF SWINDON

9.      Queenstown Bridge (Wellington Street Bridge)

| | |
|---|---|
| Grid Reference: | 151849 |
| Erected: | 1885 |
| Modified: | - |
| Demolished: | 1922/23 |
| Type: | Flat span steel road bridge with brick abutments and sheet steel sides. |
| Dimensions: | Span - 27'<br>Width - 20' |
| Remarks: | Forerunner of design for the later versions of Cambria and Whale Bridges. Built by Swindon Corporation at a cost of £900. Converted to embankment about 1922/23 when the canal was filled in. No trace remains today. Canal line now occupied by southern carriageway of Fleming Way. Site of bridge is just east of the entrance to Falcon House (Allied Dunbar Ltd) in Fleming Way. |

10.     Whale Bridge

| | |
|---|---|
| Grid Reference: | 153849 |
| Erected: | 1803/04 |
| Modified: | 1893 |
| Demolished: | 1963 |
| Type: | Original bridge was a stone arch road bridge. Reconstructed in 1893 to flat span steel bridge on brick abutments similar to (9) above. |
| Dimensions: | Original Arch span - 18' (probably)<br>Width - 15-16' (est)<br>Parapets - 44' - 45' (est)<br>1893 Version span - 25' (est)<br>Width - 36' |
| Remarks: | Original bridge which connected Princes Street and Oriel Street virtually derelict in 1893, so converted to steel bridge by Swindon Corporation at a cost of £1,200. Bridge took its name from the nearby Whale pub, which in turn was named after the old Cetus (Whale) buildings next door. A wharf was situated on the south bank, east of the bridge. Demolished during the construction of Fleming Way, |

which now occupies the canal line. No trace remains today. Site of bridge is where the two southern pedestrian subways meet in the middle of Whale Bridge roundabout.

11.     York Road Bridge (Graham Street Bridge)

| | |
|---|---|
| Grid Reference: | 157849 |
| Erected: | 1907/08 |
| Modified: | - |
| Demolished: | 1963 |
| Type: | Flat span steel road bridge with brick abutments and sheet steel sides. |
| Dimensions: | Span - 31' Width - 42' |
| Remarks: | Rather more ornate than Cambria Bridge. Built by Swindon Corporation. Broad slopes down to towpath level on north bank, probably converted to steps between 1939 and 1942. Demolished during construction of Fleming Way, which now occupies canal line. Abutments and steps on north bank down to canal level still remain, although southern abutment has been greatly shortened. |

12.     Drove Road Bridge

Grid Reference: 159849

| | |
|---|---|
| Erected: | 1803/04 |
| Modified: | - |
| Demolished: | 1921/22 |
| Type: | Stone arch road bridge. |
| Dimensions: | Arch span - 18' (probably) Width - 19' Parapets - 44' - 47' (probably) |
| Remarks: | Carried turnpike road to Cricklade. Adjacent to Swindon Wharf and Canal Manager's villa. The towpath changed banks here, being on the north bank west and on the south bank east of the bridge. Converted to embankment 1921/22 with culverts because canal still watered on either side at this time. (Canal thought to have been filled in 1922-24.) No trace remains today. Canal line indicated by Fleming Way to the west and footpath to Marsh Farm Bridge to east. |

13.     Marsh Farm Bridge (Ivy Bridge)

| | |
|---|---|
| Grid Reference: | 162850 |
| Erected: | 1804/06 |

| Modified: | - |
|---|---|
| Demolished: | Still exists |
| Type: | Stone arch access bridge |
| Dimensions: | Arch span - 18'<br>Width - 16'<br>Length of parapets - 47' |
| Remarks: | Canal beneath the bridge watered until 1973, then culverted and filled in. Oldest canal bridge in Swindon. Canal line now occupied by grassed area alongside which runs a tarmaced footpath, on the line of the former towpath. |

## 14. No name

| Grid Reference: | 165853 |
|---|---|
| Erected: | 1804/06 |
| Modified: | ? |
| Demolished: | Before 1883 |
| Type: | Probably wooden drawbridge or swing bridge. |
| Dimensions: | Not known |
| Remarks: | No trace remains today. Canal line filled in, and grassed over. Site would have been about 1/4 mile east of 13 above. |

## 15. Green Bridge

| Grid Reference: | 172860 |
|---|---|
| Erected: | 1805/06 |
| Modified: | ? |
| Demolished: | 1956/57 |
| Type: | Original bridge was probably a wooden drawbridge; may have been converted to a fixed stone bridge later (after 1920). |
| Dimensions: | Not known |
| Remarks: | Reported to be a wooden bridge in the 1920s but a stone bridge at the time of demolition. No direct information to indicate whether the former was the original bridge or a later conversion, or when, and if, the conversion to a stone bridge took place. The bridge carried a track to fields south of the canal. No trace remains today. Canal line indicated by hedgerow at the back of the gardens of Stonehurst Road to the east of A361, which is carried up to the railway bridge on an embankment |

here. The bridge would have been sited below this embankment, situated at the eastern end of the Greenbridge Industrial Estate.

### 16. Nythe Bridge (Nythe Road)

| | |
|---|---|
| Grid Reference: | 180860 |
| Erected: | 1805/06 |
| Modified: | Before 1874 |
| Demolished: | 1923/36 |
| Type: | Original bridge was probably a wooden drawbridge. Appears to have been converted to a fixed bridge before 1874. |
| Dimensions: | Not known |
| Remarks: | This bridge provided access to fields south of the canal from the Oxford road north of the canal. Demolished when the canal was filled in in the late 20s/ early 30s. Canal line lost today in the Nythe housing estate. |

### 17. No name

| | |
|---|---|
| Grid Reference: | 182860 |
| Erected: | 1805/06 |
| Modified: | - |
| Demolished: | 1914-22 |
| Type: | Probably a wooden drawbridge |
| Dimensions: | Not known |
| Remarks: | Minor access bridge similar to 16 above. Probably converted to an embankment by 1922. Canal line lost today in the Nythe housing estate. |

### 18. Stratton Wharf Bridge (Stratton Bridge)

| | |
|---|---|
| Grid Reference: | 185861 |
| Erected: | 1805/06 |
| Modified: | - |
| Demolished: | 1955/65 |
| Type: | Stone arch road bridge |
| Dimensions: | Arch span - 18' (probably)<br>Width - about 19' (probably)<br>Parapets - 44' - 47' (probably) |

Remarks:             Carried Ermin Street (the modern road built on the line of the former Roman road) across the canal. A wharf was situated on the north bank of the canal adjacent to the bridge. Date of demolition uncertain - probably early 1960s when Nythe housing estate built, and the canal filled east of the (then) A419. Site considerably altered in 1976/77 with the construction of the Stratton by-pass, and is now grassed over, just east of the end of Trajan Road, which is on the canal line west of the site. The line east of the site is indicated by the line of trees leading due east towards the by-pass and continues between double hedges beyond it.

## SECTION THREE
## NORTH WILTS CANAL FROM ITS JUNCTION WITH THE WILTS AND BERKS CANAL IN SWINDON TO MOREDON

19.    John Street Bridge (Stone Bridge)

Grid Reference:        150849

Erected:               1814

Modified:              -

Demolished:            1920/22

Type:  Stone arch road bridge

Dimensions:            Arch span - 18' (probably)
                       Width - 16' (est)
                       Length of parapets - 42' (est)

Remarks:               John Street alleged to have been named after John Harding Sheppard,
                       the owner of the land on which it was built. Had wharf adjacent (on
                       north bank) and was probably used by bargees and barge horses to
                       cross the canal if heading or coming from the east, since the canal tow-
                       path changed sides here. Demolished during infilling of canal in
                       1920/22. No trace remains today. Site would have been about 60 yds
                       west of the subway at the end of the Parade, spanning the gap between
                       Primark and Fleming Way.

20.    Fleet Street Bridge (New Bridge)

Grid Reference:        150850

Erected:               1878

Modified:              1878/85, 1885/90, 1904

Demolished:            1916

Type:                  Steel swing bridge

Dimensions:            Length of swinging portion - 32'10" Width - 15'

Remarks:               Built by Swindon Local Board. Swinging portion of bridge moved by a
                       turn table and the portion actually over the canal was only 12' long. A
                       raised footbridge (similar to those at the Golden Lion Bridge) was
                       built south of the main span before 1885, but had been removed by
                       1890. The bridge was strengthened in 1904 for the tramway, and con-
                       verted to an embankment in 1916. Site is indicated today by a slight
                       hump in the road at the junction with Fleming Way. Canal line to the
                       east is the southern carriageway of Fleming Way; to the west the line is
                       lost under new development.

21.    Bullen's Bridge (Union Canal Bridge or Sheppard's Bridge. Also known as Station Road Bridge and Cheltenham Street Bridge)

| | |
|---|---|
| Grid Reference: | 148850 |
| Erected: | 1851/52 |
| Modified: | - |
| Demolished: | 1923 |
| Type: | Steel road bridge on brick or stone abutments. Flat span with trellis work side rails. Embanked approaches. |
| Dimensions: | Span - 57' (est)<br>Width - 40' (est) |
| Remarks: | Largest canal bridge in Swindon. Thought to have been built in the USA and exhibited in the Great Exhibition of 1851 before being brought to Swindon. Alleged to be the first iron trellis bridge erected in Wiltshire. Erected by Swindon Corporation. Demolished and embanked approaches lowered and levelled in 1923. Site indicated today by hump in the road (Station Road) at the end of the cycle track/footpath from Rodbourne (Iffley Road) which is on the canal line here. |

22.    Railway Bridge (GWR Subway, also sometimes referred to as Bullen's Bridge)

| | |
|---|---|
| Grid Reference: | 147851 |
| Erected: | 1840/41 |
| Modified: | 1872, 1885/99 |
| Demolished: | Still exists |
| Type: | Original bridge was a flat span stone arch bridge. Two later widening operations used brick abutments and steel girder span supports. |
| Dimensions: | Span - about 20'<br>Width - 49'<br>First widening span - about 20'<br>First widening width - 146'<br>Second widening span - 21.5' (N) 19.5' (S)<br>Second widening width - 351' |
| Remarks: | Erected by GWR to carry main Bristol/Swindon/ Paddington line over the canal (49' wide). Widened in 1872 using brickwork and steel girders on northern side only, increasing width to 146'. Widened again on both sides by 1899, using brick work and girders to the present day width of 351'. This last widening involved the demolition of the small arch bridge (23) just to the north. Canal line indicated today by cycle track/footpath beneath the bridge. |

**23.   No name**

| | |
|---|---|
| Grid Reference: | 146852 |
| Erected: | 1814/19 |
| Modified: | - |
| Demolished: | 1885/99 |
| Type: | Stone arch access bridge |
| Dimensions: | Arch span - 18' (probably)<br>Width - 16' (est)<br>Parapets - 41' (est) |
| Remarks: | Demolished when the railway bridge (22) was widened for the second time in the period 1885 to 1899. Former site now beneath railway bridge at the northern end. |

**24.   No name**

| | |
|---|---|
| Grid Reference: | 146852 (just N of 23) |
| Erected: | 1885/99 |
| Modified: | - |
| Demolished: | 1922/42 |
| Type: | Probably a flat span steel footbridge similar to 25. |
| Dimensions: | Span - 31' (probably)<br>Width - 9' (probably) |
| Remarks: | Built by GWR as a communication bridge in the railway works. May have been built to replace the small arch bridge above (23) when the railway bridge was widened. Removed before 1942. No trace remains today. Canal line is followed by the cycle track/footpath. |

**25.   No name**

| | |
|---|---|
| Grid Reference: | 145853 |
| Erected: | 1885/99 |
| Modified: | - |
| Demolished: | 1982 |
| Type: | Flat span steel footbridge with sheet steel sides. |
| Dimensions: | Span - 31'6"<br>Width - 8'7" |
| Remarks: | Built by GWR as a communication bridge in the railway works, probably at the same time as 24. Demolished in October, 1982 and bank on eastern side of footpath landscaped, removing all trace of eastern abutment. Location of western end of bridge is still easily discernible |

by the ends of the sawn off girders at the base of the wooden fence on top of the brick wall running along the western side of the cycle track. Canal line indicated today by the cycle track/footpath from Station Road to Iffley Road which passed beneath the bridge.

**26.    No name**

| | |
|---|---|
| Grid Reference: | 60 yds S of 144855 |
| Erected: | 1978/79 |
| Modified: | - |
| Demolished: | Still exists |
| Type: | Flat span reinforced concrete road bridge on brick abutments, with steel side rails on brick parapets. |
| Dimensions: | Span - 20'10" Width - 50'4" |
| Remarks: | Built in 1978/79 to provide road link between the Hawksworth Industrial Estate west of the canal line and factories and other buildings east of the line. Steps down to the canal level footpath at SE corner. |

**27.    No name**

| | |
|---|---|
| Grid Reference: | 144855 |
| Erected: | 1885/99 |
| Modified: | - |
| Demolished: | 1914/22 |
| Type: | Probably flat span steel footbridge similar to 25. |
| Dimensions: | Probably similar to 25. |
| Remarks: | Built by GWR as a communication bridge in the railway works probably at the same time as 24 and 25. Converted to an embankment at some date between 1914 and 1922. No trace remains today. Canal line indicated by cycle track/footpath. |

**28.     Lock House Bridge**

| | |
|---|---|
| Grid Reference: | 144856 |
| Erected: | 1814/19 |
| Modified: | 1920/22 |
| Type: | Stone arch access bridge. |
| Dimensions: | Arch span - about 14' (probably)<br>Width - 14.5' (est)<br>Length of parapets - 31' (est) |

Remarks:      Provided access to Lock House adjacent to Swindon top lock. In very bad condition by 1877. Spanned the lower end of the lock chamber. Demolished during infilling by the GWR between 1920 and 1922. No trace remains today. Site would have been just west of the present day cycle track/footpath about 200 yds from the Iffley Road gasometer.

### 29.     Iffley Road Bridge

| | |
|---|---|
| Grid Reference: | 141857 |
| Erected: | 1814/19 |
| Modified: | - |
| Demolished: | 1920/22 |
| Type: | Stone arch access bridge |
| Dimensions: | Not known, but probably similar to 28. |

Remarks:      Spanned chamber of No 3 Swindon (Rodbourne) lock. In bad condition by 1877. Demolished during infilling by the GWR between 1920 and 1922. Site indicated by a slight hump in Iffley Road today, just north of the gasometer. (The embanked approaches were levelled and the road straightened in 1920/22.) Canal line south passes beneath the gasometer and northwards is indicated by the footpath to Rodbourne Road.

### 30.     Rodbourne Road Bridge (Telford Road Bridge)

| | |
|---|---|
| Grid Reference: | 138858 |
| Erected: | 1814/19 |
| Modified: | - |
| Demolished: | 1920/22 |
| Type: | Flat span steel bridge over lock chamber, with steel side rails. |
| Dimensions: | Span - about 8' (over lock chamber) <br> Width - 17'6" |

Remarks:      Spanned chamber of No 4 Swindon lock. Converted to an embankment and lock chamber filled 1920/22. No trace remains today. Site would be where the footpath from Iffley Road meets Rodbourne Road, next to the Esso filling station. Canal line indicated by this footpath east of Rodbourne Road and by the entrance road to the Cheney Manor Industrial Estate to the west.

### 31.     No name

| | |
|---|---|
| Grid Reference: | 133860 |
| Erected: | 1814/19 |
| Modified: | - |

| | |
|---|---|
| Demolished: | 1922/42 |
| Type: | Probably a wooden drawbridge |
| Dimensions: | Not known |
| Remarks: | Access bridge carrying track from south of canal to the settlement of North Leaze north of the canal. Demolished before 1942 during infilling. No trace remains today. Site would be where the service road to Shorko Films Ltd passes in front of the GEC car park, about 100 yds after leaving the main road through the industrial estate. The service road follows the canal line here. |

32.    May have been called Moredon Lock House Bridge

| | |
|---|---|
| Grid Reference | 125868 |
| Erected: | 1814/19 |
| Modified: | 1941-46? |
| Demolished: | 1948-57 |
| Type: | Probably stone or brick arch bridge with embanked approaches. |
| Dimensions: | Not known, but probably similar to Marsh Farm Bridge (13). |
| Remarks: | Carried track from west of canal east to the settlement of North Leaze, but also seems to have been built to provide a service route to Moredon Lock House just to the north. The bridge may have been converted to an embankment between 1941 and 1946, but even if it was not, the bridge was demolished during major in-filling between 1948 and 1957. |
| | Site indicated today by obvious evidence of the former embanked approach from the west, and a slightly higher level of infilling where the present day track crosses the canal line. The canal line here is well marked by double hedges, and on the west side, there is evidence of the former road or track north to the Lock House. |

33.    Railway Bridge (M & SWJR)

| | |
|---|---|
| Grid Reference: | 123873 |
| Erected: | 1883 |
| Modified: | - |
| Demolished: | 1914/22 |
| Type: | Probably flat span steel girder bridge. |
| Dimensions: | Not known |
| Remarks: | Probably a flat span bridge since the railway is on an embankment here. Converted to an embankment (probably culverted) between |

1914 and 1922. This embankment still exists today. The railway is not in use and the track has been removed.

34.     Moredon/Purton Road Bridge

Grid Reference:     122873

Erected:     1814/19

Modified:     -

Demolished:     1922/41

Type:     Probably brick or stone arch road bridge.

Dimensions:     Not known.

Remarks:     Had embanked approaches and would have had a sloping span because of higher ground to the north. Converted to an embankment by 1941. Remains as such today with canal watered on the western side of the former bridge site.

## Footnotes to Table One

## Note on Bridge Dimensions

a)     Dimensions annotated "probably" are derived from those of bridges known to be of similar type and size, for which actual dimensions are available. The annotated dimensions are not direct measurements nor is there direct evidence of their accuracy.

b)     Dimensions annotated "est" have been estimated from measurements taken from the 1886 10.56ft to the mile (1/500) Ordnance Survey plans of New Swindon.

c)     Unannotated dimensions are either direct measurements (existing bridges), or specific information derived from the Swindon Corporation bridge plans held by the Wiltshire County Records Office.

d)     For flat span bridges, the span dimension given is the distance between the abutments, not the length of the bridge superstructure.

## TABLE TWO
## SUMMARISED SEQUENCE OF INFILLING OF THE WILTS AND BERKS CANAL AND THE NORTH WILTS BRANCH IN THE SWINDON AREA 1914-1993

### 1920-1922

| | |
|---|---|
| Location: | On the North Wilts the section from the northern end of the top Swindon lock to Iffley Road (GR 143856 to 141857). |
| Remarks: | In filling carried out by GWR to provide an area for rail sidings just south of Iffley Road - hence may well have been carried out earlier than the main in filling by Swindon Corporation described below. Involved the demolition of Lock House Bridge and Iffley Road Bridge, and the filling of Nos 2 and 3 locks. |

### 1920-1923

| | |
|---|---|
| Location: | All of the canal in Central Swindon, from just south of Kingshill road (GR 141840) to Whale Bridge just east of the junction with North Wilts (GR 153849), on the main canal, and as far as Bullen's Bridge (GR 148850) on the North Wilts branch. |
| Remarks: | This was the major period of in filling just after the Great War and involved the demolition of Kingshill Road Bridge, Marlborough Street/Joseph Street footbridge, Golden Lion Bridge and Queenstown Bridge on the main canal, and of John Street Bridge on the North Wilts. (Fleet Street Bridge had already been converted to an embankment in 1916.) |
| Location: | On the main canal, the section westwards from Green Bridge (GR 172860) for about 1/2 mile to the point of entry of the Coate feeder (GR 167855). |
| Remarks: | One source(69) suggests that a dam was built across the canal at a point just east of the Coate feeder in 1919, in order to store water from Coate reservoir. The filled section ran up to this dam. 1946 aerial survey photographs indicate that another dam was built 70 yds westwards at the other end of this section to separate it from the rest of the canal and create a pool or reservoir. |
| Location: | On the North Wilts the section from just north of the main Bristol line railway bridge (GR147851) to the northern boundary of the railway works (GR 144855). |
| Remarks: | Partial filling along the eastern side of canal only. (Beyond this section, the canal remained watered to the northern end of Swindon Top Lock.) |

| | |
|---|---|
| Location: | On the North Wilts, the section from just east of Rodbourne Road (GR 138858) westward for about 380 yds to just beyond Swindon No 5 (bottom) lock. |
| Remarks: | Involved the demolition of Rodbourne Road Bridge and the filling of No 4 lock beneath the bridge. No 5 lock remained unfilled, at least up to 1922. |

## 1922 - 1925

| | |
|---|---|
| Location: | On the main canal from east of Whale Bridge (GR 153849) to Drove Road (GR 159849). |
| Remarks: | Drove Road Bridge was converted to an embankment with drainage culverts beneath in 1921/22. |
| Location: | On the North Wilts the remaining unfilled sections between Bullen's Bridge (GR 148850) and Iffley Road (GR 141357). |
| Remarks: | Bullen's Bridge demolished and levelled in 1923. |

## 1923 - 1936

| | |
|---|---|
| Location: | On the main canal, the section from Nythe Road (GR 180860) eastwards to within 300 yds of Stratton Wharf Bridge (GR 185861). |
| Remarks: | Involved the demolition of Nythe Road Bridge. The small access bridge at GR 182860 between here and Stratton Wharf Bridge is thought to have been converted to an embankment by 1922, ie, before the in filling. |
| Location: | On the main canal, the section between Green Bridge (GR 172860) and Nythe Road (GR 180860). |
| Remarks: | Partially filled. |

## 1923 - 1942

| | |
|---|---|
| Location: | On the North Wilts, the section westwards from the former site of Rodbourne Road Bridge (GR 138858) to the access bridge to North Leaze (GR 133860). |
| Remarks: | 300 yds extension westwards of the 1920/23 in filling. Involved demolition of the access bridge to North Leaze and the filling of Swindon No 5 (bottom) lock. Date uncertain. |
| Location: | On the North Wilts, the short section within the perimeter of Moredon Power Station (GR 123873 to 125873). |
| Remarks: | Probably filled when the power station was built in 1925-29. |

## 1942 - 1957

| | |
|---|---|
| Location: | On the North Wilts, the section from the former site of the access bridge to North Leaze (GR 133860) to Moredon Power Station (GR 125873). |
| Remarks: | The section immediately south of Moredon Power Station as far as Moredon top lock was probably filled between 1942 and 1946, although the lock chambers themselves were not filled until 1946-48. The remainder of this section was filled between 1948 and 1957, and during this period the access bridge at GR 125868 and Moredon Lock House were demolished. A section about 150 yds long on the western fringe of the Cheney Manor Industrial Estate at GR 128864 was left unfilled to provide a reservoir and angling facility. |
| Location: | On the North Wilts, the section between Iffley Road (GR 141357) and Rodbourne Road (GR 138858). |
| Remarks: | Filled between 1942 and 1946. |
| Location: | On the main canal a section about 250 yds long south of Kingshill Road (GR 141840). |
| Remarks: | The extension of the 1920s infill further along the line of the canal took place in at least two stages. The first stage involved an extension of about 80 yds between 1946 and 1948, whilst the remainder was filled between 1948 and 1957. |
| Location: | On the main canal, a section about 100 yds long east of Drove Road (GR 159849). |
| Remarks: | Filled in the early 1950s in preparation for the construction of Queens Drive, which was opened in 1953. |
| Location: | On the main canal, the section westwards from the point of entry of the Coate feeder (GR 167855) for a quarter of a mile. |
| Remarks: | Apart from a 70 yd long section immediately west of the feeder entry, which was retained as a reservoir for a nearby factory, this extended the 1920s in filling westwards. This reservoir was constructed prior to 1946 (probably in the early 20s) and the in filling west of it did not take place until 1948-57. |

## 1957 - 1965

| | |
|---|---|
| Location: | On the main canal, the section between Green Bridge (GR 172860) and Nythe Road (GR 180860). |
| Remarks: | This section was partially filled in 1923-1936 and completion of the in filling was necessary prior to the building of the Nythe housing estate in the early 1960s. Probably involved the demolition of Green Bridge is not already demolished earlier in the 1950s. |

| Location: | On the main canal, the section beneath Stratton Wharf Bridge (GR 185861) for about half a mile eastwards from the end of the 1923 - 1936 in fill 300 yds west of the bridge. |

| Remarks: | Probably filled in the mid 1960s with spoil from the Pressed Steel works expansion. Stratton Wharf Bridge was demolished and levelled, probably before this in filling in the late 1950s or early 1960s. |

## 1969

| Location: | On the main canal, the section from just south of the Midland and South West Junction Railway Bridge at Rushey Platt (GR 137833) south westwards to GR 136831. |

| Remarks: | This section runs through fields and the in filling is now grassed over. |

## 1973

| Location: | On the main canal, the section east of Queens Drive (GR 160849) beneath Marsh Farm Bridge to the end of the previously filled section west of the Coate feeder entry (GR 165854). |

| Remarks: | Culverted and filled, then grassed over with tarmaced footpath along the line of the former towpath (south bank). Ornamental trees planted along the in fill to provide a pleasant walk. |

## 1981 - 1982

| Location: | On the North Wilts, the section near the former site of Moredon Power Station, between the Purton Road (GR 122873) and the old M & SWJ railway (GR 123873). |

| Remarks: | A rubbish dump south of the canal was extended over the canal line in 1981 - 82. |

## 1986/87

| Location: | On the main canal, the reservoir at the western end of the Greenbridge Industrial Estate at GR167 855. |

| Remarks: | The exact date for the filling in of this reservoir is not known, but is thought to be about 1986/1987. |

## 1993

| Location: | Apart from the short section acting as reservoir a to the Cheney Manor industrial estate, the only watered sections now remaining in Swindon are the ones south of Kingshill Road at GR 128838 and the section west of the Moredon Purton road at GR 122873. |

# REFERENCES

1.    Dalby, L J             "The Wilts and Berks Canal", Oakwood Press, 1971

2.    Crittall, Elizabeth    Victoria County History of Wiltshire, Vol IX, pp 104 et seq, and Rogers, K H       Oxford University Press, 1970

3.    Smith, Martin         "Swindon and the Construction of the Wilts and Berks Canal", 1966. Thesis held in Swindon Reference Library.

4.    Fewings, J S          Letter published in Swindon "Evening Advertiser" 1967, 7th August

5.    -                      Swindon "Evening Advertiser", 1970, 21st July

6.    Dalby, L J             "The Swindon Tramways", Oakwood Press, 1973

7.    Large, F              "Swindon in Retrospect, 1856-1931", Borough Press, Swindon, 1931

8.    Grinsell, L V         "Studies in the History of Swindon", Wells, H B          Swindon Borough Council, 1950 Tallamy, H S John Betjeman

9.    Dalby, L J             Private communication, 1974

10.   Tapscott-Mason, C   Private communication, 1974

11.   Faden, W            "A Topographical Map of the County of Wilts" (2" to the mile). Published by W Faden, Geographer to HM and HRH the Prince of Wales, London. Surveyed originally in 1773 by John Adams and Andrew Drury. 2nd Edition, revised, corrected 1810.

12.   Ordnance Survey     1st Edition One Inch Ordnance Survey of England and Wales. sheet 34, Cirencester. 1820 (with railways inserted to 1891). London. (David and Charles reprint, sheet 69).

13.   Jefferies, R          "Jefferies Land, a History of Swindon and its Environs" ed Grace Toplis. Published in London 1896.

14.   Swindon            "Farewell Swindon Borough" Exhibition. An exhibition held Corporation        in Swindon Town Hall in March 1974 to mark the end of the Borough of Swindon, which was incorporated into the Borough of Thamesdown on 1st April, 1974.

15.   Blunt, R             "On Tow" - An article in Pall Mall Magazine, 1888, April, reprinted in the Inland Waterways Association Bulletin, 1966, 778, pp10-21.

16.   Dalby, L J            Private communication, 1974.

| | | |
|---|---|---|
| 17. | McNeil | Former curator, Swindon Museum (Referred to in private communication from C Tapscott-Mason) |
| 18. | - | Minutes of New Swindon Local Board Meeting of 15th March, 1898. (Referred to in private communication from C Tapscott-Mason) |
| 19. | Liddiard, N G | "The Borough of Swindon 1900-1974 being a Commemorative Essay". Published by the Borough of Swindon, March 1974 (on the occasion of its incorporation into the Borough of Thamesdown on 1st April, 1974). |
| 20. | - | Swindon Evening Advertiser, 1964, 10th August, p4. |
| 21. | The Eric Arman Collection | A collection of slides taken from old photographs and prints of Swindon, held by Swindon Museum. |
| 22. | - | Swindon Evening Advertiser, 1975, 4th July, p11 |
| 23. | - | Swindon Evening Advertiser, 1975, 7th November. |
| 24. | Harber, J | Swindon Industrial Archaeology Group, private communication, 1974. |
| 25. | - | Swindon Evening Advertiser, 1975, 21st July. |
| 26. | Bellamy, F G | Archaeology Division, Ordnance Survey, Southampton (Private Communication), 1974. |
| 27. | - | Swindon Evening Advertiser, 1962, 24th August. |
| 28. | Gibbs, W G H | Private communication, 1975. |
| 29. | Various | Comments at a meeting of the Swindon Society "The Canal as it Used to be", 10th September, 1975 |
| 30. | - | Swindon Evening Advertiser, 1975, 2nd July |
| 31. | Morris, W | "Swindon Fifty Years Ago" published in Swindon 1885 |
| 32. | - | Wilts and Berks Canal Records, No 8 Trade Ledger 1828-36 (held in Swindon Public Library) |
| 33. | Woolford, M | Private communication, 1975 |
| 34. | - | Comments of elderly members of the Queenstown Club, 1975 |
| 35. | Harris, A G | Letter to the Swindon Evening Advertiser published 1974, 30th December |
| 36. | Auerbach, J | Contribution in "A New Oarsman's Guide to the Thames", published in 1893. |
| 37. | Pullen, E | Private communication, 1974 |

| 38. | Barrett, G | Private communication, 1975 |
| 39. | - | Swindon Evening Advertiser, 1975, 29th January |
| 40. | Britton | "Topographical Sketches of North Wilts, 1826" (held by Swindon Reference Library). |
| 41. | Crittall, E | Victoria County History of Wiltshire, Vol IV, p209, Oxford University Press, 1959 |
| 42. | Hooper, W B | Private communication, 1975 (Messrs Brown and Knight Ltd) |
| 43. | Garrard Engineering | Private communication, 1976 |
| 44. | Ridge, J S | Private communication, 1975 (Messrs Walker Jackson Ltd) |
| 45. | Somerville, R | Private communication, 1976 (Messrs Garrard Engineering Ltd) |
| 46. | Dalby, L J | Private communication, 1976 |
| 47. | British Transport Historical Records Office | Private communication, 1976 |
| 48. | Alnutt, Zachary | Account of the rivers and canals west of London, 1810 |
| 49. | Wilkinson, R | Waterways World, 1974, vol 3, No 11, pp29-31 |
| 50. | ? | Harcourts "Rivers and Canals" (date not known) |
| 51. | - | Wiltshire County Records Office, Trowbridge |
| 52. | Tapscott-Mason, C | Private communication, 1977 |
| 53. | Documents C168, C169 | Swindon Library |
| 54. | Tomkins, R | Swindon Evening Advertiser, 1978, 10th February |
| 55. | - | Swindon Local History Society - slide show on the Wilts and Berks Canal, June 1979 |
| 56. | - | Kelly's Directory of Swindon, 1903 |
| 57. | Wellicome, H G D | Private communication, 1977 |
| 58. | - | Swindon Evening Advertiser, 1978, 1st September |
| 59. | - | Wiltshire Star, 1978, 13th September |
| 60. | Sheldon, P J | "Swindon in Camera - A Photographic Journey 1850-1979", Picton Publishing, 1979 |
| 61. | - | Member of the audience at a slide show presented at the Arts Centre, Devizes Road, Swindon, by Mr P Boyce, Wilts and Berks Canal Amenity Group, on 22nd February, 1979. |

| 62. | - | Swindon Evening Advertiser, 1977, 21st July (Information in this article attributed to Mrs R Cable and Mr S Perry). |
|---|---|---|
| 63. | Hurwitz, S | Swindon Evening Advertiser, 1977, 12th July |
| 64. | Hamley, B | Letter published in Swindon Evening Advertiser, 1967, 7th August. |
| 65. | Jefferies, Joan | Letter published in Swindon Evening Advertiser, 1978, 7th February. |
| 66. | Huby, J | Swindon Evening Advertiser, 1979, 6th February. |
| 67. | - | Wiltshire Star, 1978, 15th March |
| 68. | "Moonraker" | Swindon Evening Advertiser, 1978, 17th February. |
| 69. | May, R W | Private communication, 1978 |
| 70. | Meader, Mrs B J | Letter published in the Wiltshire Star, 1978, 1st November. |
| 71. | - | Wiltshire Star, 1978, 11th October. |
| 72. | Bampton, Daphne | Letter published in Swindon Evening Advertiser, 1977, 1st November. |
| 73. | Hurwitz, S | Swindon Evening Advertiser, 1977, 13th July. |
| 74. | - | Swindon Evening Advertiser, 1977, 16th June. |
| 75. | Lewis, A S | Letter published in Swindon Evening Advertiser, 1977, 29th June. |
| 76. | May, R W | Article published in Swindon Evening Advertiser, 1978, 12th April. |
| 77. | Tull, Mrs D | Private communication, 1979 |
| 78. | James, H G | Letter published in Swindon Evening Advertiser, 1979, 25th July. |
| 79. | - | Swindon Evening Advertiser, 1978, 4th July |
| 80. | - | Swindon Evening Advertiser, 1954, 14th September |
| 81. | Coole, W L | Private communication, 1979 |
| 82. | Dunn, Mrs D | Private communication, 1979 |
| 83. | Jones, S K | Private communication, 1979 |
| 84. | RAF Aerial Survey 1946 | Print No 4325, taken 16th April 1946, Ref: 106G/UK/1416 |
| 85. | RAF Aerial Survey 1948 | Print Nos 5115, 5116, 5117, taken 11th March 1948, Ref: CPE/UK/2490 |

| 86. | RAF Aerial Survey 1948 | Print Nos 5124, 5125, 5139, taken 11th March 1948, Ref: CPE/UK/2490 |
| 87. | RAF Aerial Survey 1948 | Print Nos 5125, 5138, taken 11th March 1948 REF: CPE/UK/2490 |
| 88. | RAF Aerial Survey 1948 | Print Nos 5129, 5135, 5136, taken 11th March 1948, Ref: CPE/UK/2490 |
| 89. | RAF Aerial Survey 1946 | Print No 4082, taken 16th April 1946, Ref: 106G/UK/1416 |
| 90. | RAF Aerial Survey 1948 | Print Nos 5134, 5135, taken 11th March 1948, Ref CPE/UK/2490 |
| 91. | RAF Aerial Survey 1946 | Print Nos 3083, 3084, taken 14th April 1946, Ref: 106G/UK/1416 |
| 92. | RAF Aerial Survey 1948 | Print Nos 5157, 5158, taken 11th March 1948, Ref CPE/UK/2490 |
| 93. | RAF Aerial Survey 1946 | Print Nos 3085, 3086, taken 14th April 1946, Ref: 106G/UK/1416 |
| 94. | RAF Aerial Survey 1946 | Print No 3678, taken 16th April 1946, Ref: 106G/UK/1416 |
| 95. | RAF Aerial Survey 1948 | Print No 5170, taken 11th March 1948, Ref: CPE/UK/2490 |
| 96. | - | Swindon Evening Advertiser, 1981, 20th November. |
| 97. | Howell, Michael A | "Bygone Swindon", Phillimore & Co, 1984, (published on behalf of the Swindon Society). |
| 98. | Peck, Alan S | "The Great Western at Swindon Works", Oxford Publishing Co, 1983 |
| 99. | Backhouse, David W | "Home Brewed - A History of Brewing and Public Houses in North Wiltshire", 2nd Edition, published by CAMRA (Swindon Branch), 1985 |
| 100. | Dorling, Mrs L | Private Communication, 1990 |
| 101. | Darnell, Victor C | "Nathaniel Rider and his Iron Bridges", Kensington, Connecticut, U.S.A., 1990. |

# LIST OF ILLUSTRATIONS

| Figure No | Description | Page |
|---|---|---|
| 1 | Swindon Street Plan c. 1945 | 6 |
| 2 | New Swindon, 1849 | 12 |
| 3 | Railway Village 1860s | 13 |
| 4 | Webb's Timber Yard and Warehouse, Cambria Bridge Wharf, 1880s | 15 |
| 5 | Cambria Bridge Wharf 1880s | 16 |
| 6 | Orlando Baker's 1882 Map of Swindon | 17 |
| 7 | Rushey Platt Railway Bridge, June 1991 | 16 |
| 8 | Milton Road Bridge, February 1972 | 20 |
| 9 | Cambria Bridge, November 1975 (Built 1893) | 23 |
| 10 | Tram approaching Golden Lion Bridge 1905 | 26 |
| 11 | Junction with the North Wilts Canal and Golden Lion Bridge, c 1911 | 28 |
| 12 | Central Club and Milton Road Bridge, April 1975 | 34 |
| 13 | Canal Milestone, Canal Walk, June 1991 | 37 |
| 14 | Golden Lion, Canal Walk, June 1978 | 38 |
| 15 | Present Day Cambria Bridge (reconstructed 1978), June 1991 | 39 |
| 16 | Present Day Milton Road Bridge (renovated 1981), November 1981 | 39 |
| 17 | View from Cambria Bridge looking towards the Centre of Swindon, November 1975 | 43 |
| 18 | The Parade (now Canal Walk), March 1972 | 45 |
| 19 | Site of Former Junction with North Wilts Canal, May 1972 | 46 |
| 20 | York Road Bridge, c 1912 | 56 |
| 21 | Swindon Wharf c 1914 | 57 |
| 22 | Marsh Farm Bridge, June 1991 | 66 |
| 23 | View East from Wiltshire Hotel along Canal Line, April 1974 | 69 |
| 24 | Northern Abutment of York Road Bridge, April 1974 | 72 |
| 25 | Aerial Photograph of Canal Line near the County Ground, 1963 | 71 |
| 26 | Golden Lion Bridge Mural, Medgbury Road, September 1976 | 74 |

27    Plan of the GWR Works, Swindon, 1846                                    77

28    Sheet XV 421 Ordnance Survey 10.56 ft/mile Series (surveyed
      1885), Central Swindon                                                  82

29    Sheet XV 315 Ordnance Survey 10.56 ft/mile Series (surveyed
      1885), The Canal through the GWR Works                                  83

30    John Street Bridge, c 1914                                              86

31    GWR Footbridge and Station Road/ Iffley Road Cycle Track/
      Footpath, March 1974                                                    88

32    Bullen's Bridge, 1923                                                   92

33    New Bridge over Station Road/Iffley Road Cycle Track/
      Footpath , June 1991                                                    96

34    View North from the 7th Floor of the AUEW Building, May 1972     99

35    Start of Cycle Track/Footpath from Station Road to Iffley Road,
      May 1972                                                               100

36    Cleared Out Section of Canal at the Rear of Shorko Films Ltd,
      Rodbourne Industrial Estate, March 1972                               102

# ERRATA

| | |
|---|---|
| **CONTENTS** | Section 1 - History<br>1914 to the present  -  Page number - alter to 29. |
| **Page 5** | Last para, first line - 14th word should be "one". |
| **Page 10** | Last para, third line - 3rd word should be "1867". |
| **Page 18** | Third para, last line - Cross reference for Fig. 28 should be to page 82, not 84. |
| **Page 40** | First para, first line -  10th word  Substitute "to" for "and". |
| **Page 41** | Sixth para, first line - 12th word should be "span". |
| **Page 97** | Last line - 9th word should be "built". |
| **Page 110** | First line - delete "9.". |
| **Page 119** | Bridge No. 28, Lock House Bridge.<br>In the description of this bridge, for the word "Modified", substitute "Demolished". |
| **Page 132** | Fig 3 - date should be 1885.<br>Fig 24 - page number should be 70. |

**- oOo -**

# Instant Pot

## Cookbook for Beginners 2024

*1800* Days Daily Instant Pot Recipes with Full-colour Pictures, Simplify Your Kitchen Routine and Enjoy Nourishing and Quality Meals

Helen J. Hill